Off Rhythm

Aprıl Adams

Published by Lechner Syndications

www.lechnersyndications.com

ISBN 13: 978-1-927794-27-2

"When I go in to compete, whether it's gymnastics or anything else, I do my own thing. I compete with myself."

- Shannon Miller

CONTENTS

CHAPTER 1

"One. Two. Three!" Kelley and her best friend Jamie gave one giant tug and dragged their two-person kayak through the sand and onto the beach.

"Oh my gosh, that was so much fun!" exclaimed Jamie as both girls collapsed onto the sand beside the lake.

"Next time, we have to kayak all the way to the little island," Kelley said.

Jamie lifted her head just enough to see the island in the distance. "It's a good thing we have gymnastics muscles," she laughed. "Kayaking is not as easy as it looks!" Then she caught sight of a lone kayak still on the water. "Wow. Your brother is still out there."

Kelley smiled. "My brother is still out there because he likes the girl whose family rents the cottage on the other side of the lake." Both girls giggled. "He's only two years older than we are, but he's definitely moved beyond the *girls are gross* phase."

"Well, girls are definitely NOT gross." Jamie looked over at Kelley and smiled mischievously. "And I don't think boys are gross either. I'm just not ready to paddle across a whole lake just to see one!"

"Yea!" Kelley agreed. "Even if we do have killer gym muscles!"

The girls continued to lie on their backs and stare up at the late summer sky. Kelley's cheeks were already pink and freckled from a day out in the sun, while Jamie's skin had deepened into a golden-bronze after a summer of swimming, kayaking, and biking outdoors. Kelley

1

reached over and pulled on one of her friend's long spiral curls, wishing briefly that her own straight brown hair looked so good in the humidity.

"Can you believe it's Labor Day already?" Jamie said, out of the blue.

Kelley pushed herself up on her elbows and studied the scene. She loved her grandma's summer house with its big beautiful outdoor patio looking over the best lake in the world with the most fun dock and slide ever. It wasn't that far from Seattle, but it always felt like an entirely different world.

"I'm really glad you could come to the lake with us," Kelley said as she turned her head to look at her best friend. Jamie looked super-calm and content as always. She was the most fun-loving, low-stress person Kelley knew, and she was grateful for Jamie's positive energy both at the gym and when they were just hanging out. Jamie was wearing a turquoise one-piece with red swirls that Kelley had given her at the beginning of the summer. Jamie lived with her mom and grandma and money was sometimes tight, so Kelley loved when she could share her favorite outfits with her best friend.

Kelley's swimsuit was a bright yellow and orange suite that the girls had found on super-sale during one of their typical Friday night trips to the mall. They almost never bought anything more than ice cream, but they loved the ritual of knowing they'd get to spend stress-free time together at the end of every hard week of gymnastics training.

"I can't imagine a more perfect way to end the summer," Kelley said. "Even if I am more tired than if we'd just competed at Nationals!"

Jamie smiled at the memory of their last major competition before summer break. "We so rocked Nationals last spring. I can't wait to see what our squad is going to do this year!"

Kelley grinned. She could almost tell what Jamie was thinking just by watching the shifts in her facial expressions. Jamie had been so determined to master a special dismount on vault at their Nationals competition in Salt Lake City, Utah last spring that she through it in unplanned at the last second and ended up flubbing the dismount entirely. She lost an entire tenth of a point. Still, Kelley thought it was pretty cool that her friend had been willing to try something so risky at such a major competition. Jamie had wanted to set herself apart from the rest of the competition and in Kelley's opinion, she had. Even with that one major mistake, Jamie still managed to place fourth on beam and sixth on floor. Not bad for their first National competition.

Jamie turned to face Kelley. "Your floor routine was amazing. You know that, right?"

Kelley blushed. The truth was, she did know it. She had convinced the squad's choreographer, Max to mash-up her typical country music score with a little bit of a hip hop beat and the unusual pairing had the audience on their feet and stomping along. For her second dance pass, he'd choreographed a unique combination of the running man and the do-si-do that even got a few people in the audience hooting and whistling. Even though Kelley hadn't earned a spot on the podium, she was still very proud of that performance. She loved the way floor allowed her to show off the strength in her legs that she'd built up from years of soccer and the graceful, limber movements she'd mastered in her dance classes. If she thought about it, floor was really her favorite part of gymnastics. And beam. And being with her squad-mates, who were also amazing at competition.

"Kips rule!" both girls said at the same time. "Jinx!"

The sound of a door slamming grabbed both girls' attention. They sat up just as Kelley's mom and grandma came out of the house.

"Looks like your mom and grandma are going for a walk," Jamie said.

Kelley jumped to her feet. "Maybe we can convince them to stop for ice cream on the way back."

"Race you!" Jamie took off knowing full well that no matter how much of a head start she got, Kelley would pass her. There was no competing with a gymnast who also happened to be an amazing soccer player *and* an incredible dancer. Kelley's legs were lightning fast!

"Hey!" Kelley called out to her mom and grandma. "You guys want some company?"

"We have company," her grandma smiled. "I think what you really mean is *wouldn't you like some ice cream?*"

"Why yes we would!" Jamie nodded. "Thanks for asking!"

The girls linked arms as they joined up with the older women.

Before long, they had pulled ahead by just enough to give them the privacy they needed to talk.

"I wish we didn't go to different schools," Jamie said. "It would be so great to have classes together."

"I know," Kelley agreed, "but at least practices are starting up again. You'll see me every day anyway."

Suddenly, Jamie stopped short. She was staring up ahead of them. Kelley followed her gaze.

Just ahead on the road was a little cottage and in the yard was a girl about their age doing something that looked like a cross between gymnastics and dance. She held a hula hoop, but she was hardly using it like Kelley was used to seeing a hula hoop be used.

The girl threw the hoop into the air and then leaped into a grand jeté with perfect extension before landing just in time to catch the hoop effortlessly. Then, she did an aerial cartwheel while holding the hoop only to then throw it high into the air so she could spin through a triple pirouette before catching it again.

Kelley gasped as the girl caught the hoop like it was the easiest thing in the world. *This is so beautiful,* thought Kelley. She could watch forever!

"Whoa," Jamie whispered. "That's a*mazing!*"

Kelley nodded, in awe, "it's like the perfect combination of ballet and gymnastics!"

Kelley remembered her partnering classes at the ballet studio and how wonderful it felt to be truly connected to someone while you were dancing. As she watched the girl roll from a backbend into a chin-stand, all the while twirling the hoop on her arm and then her leg, it looked like she was dancing with the perfect partner. The girl and the hoop were absolutely connected. They moved separately and together at the same time. Her movements were exciting and athletic like gymnastics but also graceful and elegant, like ballet.

What Kelley loved most was how confident and fearless this girl appeared, as if there wasn't a chance in the world she would injure herself. Kelley had grown so much more cautious since doing gymnastics. Injuries played such a big role on being able to participate. She'd nearly had to skip Nationals last year because of a sprained ankle and her squad-mate, Sara, had broken both wrists just by doing a simple back tuck and her back tumbles were never the same again.

But this wonderful combination of gymnastics and dance looked so much less threatening even though Kelley knew how hard it was to look so effortless. The girl moved with clean lines and was clearly every bit as toned as Kelley and Jamie.

"She's totally a gymnast," said Jamie. "This is rhythmic gymnastics, right?"

"You mean like what Bethany does?" Kelley felt a twinge of guilt as she spoke the name of their former squad-mate and friend. Competitive gymnastics had proven too much for Bethany. A sudden growth spurt left her feeling too tall to be graceful on vault and even though she was incredibly graceful and talented on the floor routine, the pressure of the vault, uneven bars, and beam was just too much for her. So she'd left the squad last year to start training for Cirque du Soleil. Bethany and Kelley had been such great friends, but they'd lost touch now that they were no longer on the same squad.

"I don't think so," Jamie said. "There's no competition with what Bethany does. Rhythmic gymnastics is totally competitive. I mean, it's in the Olympics. You could win a Gold Medal doing that!"

Jamie's words sent a shiver down Kelley's spine. "Right..." Kelley whispered. She couldn't help envisioning herself standing atop that three-tiered podium.

"Hello?" Jamie whispered, as she elbowed Kelley, "did you just see that?"

Kelley snapped her attention back to the girl just as she threw herself into a windmilling leg extension that positioned her pointed toe exactly opposite from the tip of her head. Her pointed leg spun in opposition to her shoulders and head so that when her foot reached straight up to the sky, her head was almost touching the floor and vice versa. At the same time, the hoop spun perfectly on her arm. Kelley could barely breathe from the excitement of what she was seeing. So when the girl suddenly let go the hoop at the top of an arc so that it floated high into the air while she whipped herself around in a series of fouetté turns, Kelley couldn't help but shout in approval.

The girl suddenly stopped as the hoop came falling down to the ground. Jamie and Kelley's mom and grandma broke into a round of applause.

"I'm so sorry," Kelley said as the girl approached her. "I didn't mean to interrupt you. I just—wow!"

The girl blushed a little through her dark tan and smattering of freckles. "That's okay!" she said, tucking a short curl behind her ear. "I didn't even realize you were there!"

Kelley couldn't help but notice the girl's wonderfully bright green eyes that sparkled when she talked. She liked her immediately.

"I'm Jamie and this is Kelley," Jamie said. "We do gymnastics too but nothing like that. That was amazing!"

Kelley smiled as she stepped back to watch Jamie do her thing. It was impossible not to admire how friendly and outgoing she was. It was the first thing Kelley had noticed about her last year when she moved to town from Miami. It was her unique combination of determination and friendliness that helped her find her place so quickly on the squad. It was as if she'd always been a Kip.

"My name's Cadence," the girl said.

"That was quite impressive," Kelley's mom said. "Where did you learn to do that?"

"Oh, my mom teaches rhythmic gymnastics," Cadence said. "She's been testing out new routines and choreography on me since I was four years old."

"But I also feed you and buy you cool clothes!" Cadence's mom appeared through the door of the cabin. "It's not all slave labor!"

Cadence laughed and Kelley and Jamie followed her example.

"I just made some fresh watermelon juice in the blender," her mom said, "It's a little bit of an experiment, but why don't you join us?"

Kelley's mom and grandma stepped up toward the porch.

"I'm Gail," Cadence's mom said as she held out her hand and led them into the kitchen.

Kelley and Jamie followed Cadence to the flat back lawn where her dad was already building a bonfire. The end of the day was putting a chill in the air—another reminder that summer was at an end.

"So where do you guys do gymnastics?" Cadence asked as she mindlessly continued to stretch her legs.

"We're Kips!" Jamie explained and then as if to demonstrate what she'd said, she took off on a tumbling pass that included a front walkover, aerial cartwheel, and a forward flip.

"Very nice!" Cadence laughed.

Kelley applauded Jamie's always-great form but shied away from joining her. She didn't want to start the season off with an injury.

"So how would that move be different in rhythmic gymnastics?"

"Well, for one," Cadence replied, "there is always music. And two, we don't do tumbling runs *but* if we did, it would be while twirling a ribbon in a perfect swirl or throwing a couple of clubs up in the air!"

"No way!" Jamie exclaimed.

"It sounds hard at first, but you get used to it. Especially if you happen to be a multitasker! You definitely have to be able to do two things at once in rhythmic, but the trade-off is that a lot of the moves are not as intense as straight gymnastics, because you have the props to deal with instead."

"Girls! We're making s'mores!" Cadence's dad called out to them.

"My mom can tell you more," Cadence said as they headed over to the fire just Cadence's mom, Gail, arrived with the marshmallows. Kelley's mom and grandma carried the chocolate and graham crackers.

"So I hear you girls are Kips," Gail said. "Very impressive! You did extremely well at Nationals last year. Cadence and I were there watching, even though we weren't competing at that point. We loved being spectators."

"Not anymore though," Cadence chimed in. "Mom's starting a new squad. There are a bunch of us that have been doing Rhythmic for a long time but only recreationally. Now we're finally going to form a team and compete!"

"Really?" Kelley said, unable to hide her interest. "How do the competitions work?"

"Well, one of the biggest differences," said Gail, "is that rhythmic gymnasts can perform group routines as well as solos."

"You mean, you get to perform together at the same time? Like in dance?" Kelley so missed being part of an ensemble like she'd been in ballet, before she gave it up to compete at a higher level in gymnastics. And soccer too! She liked competing with the Kips and helping the squad to a win but in some ways, gymnastic competitions were as much *against* your fellow squad-mates as it was *with* them. Plus, every performance was a solo, which was very stressful. Kelley missed being part of a team that really worked together like dancers and soccer players.

"Earth to Kelley!" Jamie tugged on her sleeve.

"Sorry," Kelley smiled. "Guess I drifted off for a second."

"Kelley used to be a dancer," Jamie said.

Used to be, Kelley thought to herself. The words bugged her. She didn't want to be a person who "used to" do anything.

"Kelley! Oh, man! Rhythmic would be so great for you!" Jamie declared. "You'd be a total natural! Its dance and gym combined! You'd be amazing!"

Kelley stared at Jamie in amazement, as if she'd been reading her mind.

"We're doing a demo at the Seattle City Center next Saturday," said Gail. "You girls should come."

Kelley and Jamie exchanged looks.

"Saturday is our first day back at the gym," Jamie said, a little disappointed, as if that meant they couldn't go.

Kelley felt her stomach sink. Then she had a brilliant idea.

"That's okay," she insisted. "We'll bring the whole team!"

CHAPTER 2

Kelley practically skipped into the gym on Saturday morning. She was super excited to be back for the year. The first day of school was fun and she got to see all her old friends and soccer teammates, but there was nothing better than the smell of the gym—or the *lack* of smell in her new leotard and gym bag. *That's the best part of a new year,* she thought. *My clothes and bag don't reek of sweat and chalk yet!*

Jamie raced up to her before she had even put her things down.

"It's a new year!" Jamie squealed and she nearly lifted Kelley off the ground with a hug.

Kelley looked around at all the other familiar faces. Sara was back full time after a struggle with stress-related OCD. Even Nadia was happy to see her.

"We've got a good squad this year," Nadia said. "Raven will be back from visiting her dad next week. And Sara's back in top form on the uneven bars. As is my mom. She's already had me practicing my split leap on the balance beam in our basement."

"I still can't believe you have a beam in your basement!" said Jamie. "I practice on the couch cushions."

Kelley took a step back to watch her friends happily chatting as they stretched out for practice. Kelley had always loved this moment when everyone clicked into place before the real hard work and competition began. When they were just friends who loved the same activity and wanted each other to be the best they could each be.

"So listen," Jamie said getting everyone's attention. "After practice, Kelley and I are going to watch a rhythmic gymnastics demo." Jamie recounted the whole story of meeting Cadence in hopes of convincing the rest of the girls to join them.

"Aren't they forbidden to do tumbling runs?" asked Sara.

"Sounds like baby gymnastics to me," said Nadia.

"You're right. I've never seen anyone but a baby able to pull their leg up past their head!" Jamie was the only one who ever got away with calling Nadia out on her harsh comments or hyper-competitive moments. "Anyway, it's beautiful and you guys are going to love it!"

"*Aaaaaannnnd,*" said Kelley as she wrapped one arm around Nadia and the other around Sara, "my mom said she'd drive us and promised that we could stop for ice cream sundaes afterward."

Nadia lifted her chin up a little higher as if offended by the offer. "You know I cannot be bribed with creamy dairy desserts with fudgy toppings."

"I can!" Sara said, zipping up her sweat jacket. "How soon do we leave?"

****

The first practice flew by. It was tough work getting back to the discipline and rigor of a Kips training session, but it was great to be back with everybody. Even so, Kelley was really excited to be sitting in the family Surburban and headed toward the Rhythmic demo. She couldn't wait to see more of it. Even better, Jamie had worked her magic on the squad and everyone was piling into the car to go with them.

Kelley sat in the front seat and gave each of her ankles a quick stretch. She drew the alphabet with her feet to make sure she stretched everything fully. She was determined to have an injury-free season.

"This had better be interesting," Nadia said. "We have an intense season coming up. We can't afford to waste time."

"It's always an excellent idea to watch other gymnasts in action," said Sara.

"If you can call them gymnasts," Nadia muttered.

Kelley's stomach did an involuntary flip. She remembered how she'd gotten so nervous at one of her earliest competitions that she'd overstepped on a landing and fallen right on her butt in front of an entire auditorium full of people.

"Remember how you came in sixth overall on beam at Nationals, Kell?" Jamie could always tell when Kelley was stressing, and strangely, what she was stressing about.

"We're going to have a really solid team for the group all-around this year," said Nadia, in an uncharacteristic moment of positivity.

When they arrived at the high school where the demo was going to happen, the girls found a gym packed with rows and rows of folding tables, each featuring an extracurricular activity for the fall. There were kids everywhere signing up for endless activities. Soccer clubs, football, karate, piano, theater arts, yoga—it was Kelley's best and worst nightmare at the same time. She never met an activity that didn't look like fun. She was heading toward a table featuring yoga ball basketball when she heard her name being called across the room. She looked up to see her old soccer coach waving at her. She jumped up and down and waved back. Kelley loved the buzz of the gym. All the possibilities.

"This is so cool!" she shouted to Jamie over the din of so many kids shouting and racing around. "I want to do everything please!"

"Stay focused!" Jamie said as she pulled her through the crowd. "Remember your mom!"

Jamie was right. Kelley's mom had been totally supportive of all her interests until last year. She had always said that Kelley had her whole life to focus on one thing that she should test out as many things as she could while she was young. But last year had been the breaking point. Her schedule just got too full and her mom finally said she had to start making some choices. That's when she cut back on ballet and soccer to do gymnastics.

"Wow!" Kelley exclaimed as Jamie dragged her through the gym. "Did you know you could take archery lessons at the Rec center?"

"Just what we need," Nadia said, "spearing yourself in the foot before the next competition."

"Bocce Ball!" Kelley called out as they passed another table.

Her teammates all groaned at once.

"Keep her moving!" cried Nadia.

"You guys could so totally be messing with my future right now. I might be great at Bocce Ball and now I'll never know!" Kelley argued through her laughter.

"Hey look!" Sara exclaimed. "Free Vitamin Water!" The group descended on the table and each got their free sample before heading over to the area where the rhythmic gymnastics demo would happen. They sat next to each other on the ground just as the announcer introduced Cadence's mom.

Kelley felt a round of butterflies in her stomach as Gail took the microphone and welcomed the crowd to their Rhythmic demo. She couldn't wait to see more Rhythmic.

"We are very excited to have this opportunity to give you a glimpse into what rhythmic gymnastics is," she said. "This is a sport that allows athletes to compete both as soloists and team members. Some of it might look familiar to you and some of it might seem brand new. It is gymnastics but it's also a lot of dance. And the part that might seem a little new to you is the fact that we use props—a ball, a hoop, a ribbon, a club, or a rope. I think I'll let our demonstration do the rest of the explaining. But I do want to let you know that we are forming a new team this fall so if any of you find this interesting, I hope you'll come see me afterwards. Enjoy!"

"Dance, gymnastics, and there's a ball just like soccer. It's your perfect sport!" Jamie whispered to Kelley as Gail walked off the stage.

"Sounds like the circus," Nadia said.

"It takes serious strength and power, Nadia," Jamie defended. "Flexibility, agility, dexterity, endurance, eye-hand coordination—"

"Toys!" added Nadia.

"Shhh!" Kelley said, not even caring that she was shushing Nadia. Her full attention was on the stage.

A petite blond girl stepped up to the mat for the first solo carrying a shiny gold ball, about half the size of a basketball. A huge braid flowed from the top of her head and she wore a gold and cream bodysuit with a skirt.

"She's so pretty!" Jamie whispered to Kelley.

"She needs to be," whispered Nadia, "if she's going to insist on walking around with that silly gold ball."

Jamie shot Nadia a look. Nadia went silent, but not without a smirk.

The blonde girl did a double pirouette and tossed the ball ten feet up into the air as she rolled onto the ground and caught the ball between her ankles.

Kelley couldn't help but applaud as the routine continued. The girl threw and caught the ball in so many amazing ways as she continued to dance and do gymnastic moves just like the Kips would do.

How could Nadia not be impressed with that routine? thought Kelley, as she applauded. *It was amazing!*

Cadence was up next. She wore a blue-green outfit that made her eyes sparkle even more than usual.

"I love that costume!" whispered Kelley. "So much more elaborate than the basic leotards we wear in competition."

The girls sat in amazement as Cadence flicked the long ribbon so that it slithered like a snake or looped around her like a lasso, all the while doing complicated twists and many of the aerial elements the girls knew so well. Her lines were just as lean and strong as when Jamie and Kelley had seen her perform on the beach, but this time she knew she was performing and the intensity of her focus and the beauty of grace shone through even more.

She ended her routine with the same grand jeté she had done by the lake, but her extension was even more impressive and her height was unbelievable. And, through it all, the ribbon continued to float above her in a perfect circle.

"Wow!" Kelley whispered.

"I don't think even you could do that, Nadia," Jamie joked.

"She looks like a ballerina trying to lasso a gymnast," Nadia muttered, but clearly she was more impressed than she wanted to be.

"That doesn't even make sense," Sara whispered.

"Whatever," Nadia replied.

The last solo was performed by an east-Indian girl wearing a red outfit that complemented the soft brown tones of her complexion. Her leotard sparkled in the light and reminded Kelley of the beautiful costumes she wore in her dance recitals. The girl held a hoop just like the one Cadence had used. The music began and the girl lifted her leg so that her calf was nearly at her ear and in that position she threw the hoop and caught it with her foot where it floated as it spun in circles around her ankle.

"Oh my god, this makes me miss dance so much!" Kelley whispered to Jamie.

Kelley watched the last performance with such a longing in her gut. She hadn't realized just how deeply she missed dance until she saw the Rhythmic Gymnasts. There was no replacing the feeling of peaceful calm she felt when she was mid-dance. How was it possible that feeling so calm could also feel so exciting at the same time? Kelley was so lost in her own thoughts that the applause startled her. She looked up to see all three girls running out on to the stage with Cadence right in the center of it all.

"Are they going to perform together now?" Jamie asked.

"Oh, joy," murmured Nadia.

"Shh," Sara silenced her. Her attention was focused with none of her usual fidgeting. Kelley was impressed. Usually, if Sara wasn't training or doing homework, she was stressing out. *This must seem like training to her,* thought Kelley.

Kelley looked back to the stage. Each of the girls wore a shimmering golden green outfit. They looked like beautiful exotic jungle creatures. The music began. A haunting sound cued the girls to begin circling each other with the grace of birds flying in formation. They each carried two clubs that looked like slender, light bowling pins. At once, all the girls tossed one club into the air as they fell into a back roll, stood, and caught their club as it came down. No one flinched. No one missed a beat. It was like one person moving with half a dozen perfect reflections.

"Whoa," said Jamie. "I don't know if our squad could be so synchronized."

In spite of herself, Nadia nodded in agreement.

Each of the movements was precise and each girl made them at the exact same time in the exact same way. At one point, they each tossed one of their clubs in the air, did a series of quick turns that moved them in a circle so that they each caught another girl's club as it fell back down.

Kelley wondered if she, Jamie, Sara, and Nadia could ever move exactly alike. They were all so different with such different styles. It didn't seem possible, but here were these girls, one super petite, another curvy, all moving as one.

As the performance ended, all the girls broke into applause—even Nadia.

"That was incredible!" Jamie exclaimed.

"Uh-huh." Kelley didn't know what else to say. She just felt she needed to be up there doing it too.

"Let's go find Cadence and congratulate her," Jamie said as she led her squad through the crowd.

Gail saw the girls as they approached the edge of the stage.

"Jamie! Kelley! I'm so glad you made it!" Gail said as she held out fliers. "And you brought your squad!"

Cadence came running when she saw them.

"You were so beautiful," Kelley said quietly as she hugged Cadence. "So amazing!"

"Would you girls like to try a free class?" Gail asked.

"No," said Nadia, bluntly.

Sara jabbed a finger into Nadia's side. "What my friends means to say, is no thank you. We're all pretty busy with our gymnastics training, but thank you very much for the offer. And the demo was really cool."

Kelley wanted desperately to reach for a flier but it suddenly felt like a betrayal to her squad. Instead she stood silently as everyone around her carried on about the performance. Kelley replayed each amazing move in her mind.

As Sara, Jamie, and Nadia turned to leave, Kelley quickly took a flier and shoved it in her bag. But Nadia had turned back and seen her.

"As if you need another distraction," she said, rolling her eyes.

"Just being polite – you should try it sometime," Kelley replied and ran ahead to join the other girls.

****

When the Suburban was finally empty of all her friends, Kelley sat quietly with her mother. It took her several blocks to work up the nerve to speak. Finally, she took a deep breath and said, "I want to try Rhythmic."

Her mom raised an eyebrow but let her keep talking.

"It combines dance and gym and there's no vault—you know how I hate vault—and dance... Mom, I didn't realize how much I miss dance!"

Kelley's longing hung in the air as her mom pulled the car into the driveway, put it in park and turned off the ignition before turning to face her daughter.

"You already know where I stand on extracurricular activities. This is an either/or situation. This is not an additional activity."

Kelley nodded. She did understand. It wouldn't be an easy decision. But she had to find out if Rhythmic was her thing. "I just have to try it, Mom. I have to see if it feels like dance."

Because if it does, Kelley thought, *then it's perfect!*

CHAPTER 3

"Kip. Kip"

"Hooray!"

"Kip. Kip."

"Hooray!"

Decked out in their black and fuchsia practice leotards, the four Bellevue Kips gave one last chant to close out an excellent practice session.

Kelley's muscles ached from the first days back after so much time off. The workouts were even more intense than she remembered, but she felt stronger every day. She felt capable. And, getting back on the tumble track, flying through the air, that was just pure fun! So why was she left with a queasy pit in her stomach as her squad-mates headed to the locker room? Why did everything have to feel so unsettled? She loved artistic gymnastics. She was good at it. It would be so much easier to just stick with it. Why did she even feel as if she needed to try something new?

But it was as if she had awoken a sleeping beast inside her. From the moment she saw Cadence leaping and spinning—dancing—nothing had been the same. She desperately wanted to go to the free rhythmic trial class tomorrow just to feel what it was like to mix dance and gym. But that would mean missing a practice, and she couldn't do that without getting her coach's permission. It was still early in the season and nowhere near the run-up to competition so it shouldn't be a problem, but Kelley had a history with Coach Judi about missing practices. It stretched back to the time when she used to miss so many practices because of soccer and dance.

Kelley studied Judi from across the gym. She was consulting with Max, their choreographer. *She's probably planning this season's floor routines,* Kelley thought. Then she flashed on the country-western medley she'd been given last year for her floor routine. She really hoped for something a little less hokey this year!

She forced her feet to start moving toward her coach. She just had to do it, tell Judi that she couldn't be there tomorrow. *It's not such a huge deal,* Kelley told herself.

She felt her confidence weakening with every step, like the air being slowing let out of a balloon. But she kept walking.

Judi looked up from her clipboard when Kelley got near. Kelley could already feel suspicion rising up in her coach. It was all over her face.

"Good work on beam today, Kel! Nice long lines. Good arm strength. Seems like the time off this summer was just what the doctor ordered—time to heal your injuries."

"Yes," Kelley said. "About that." She started to stutter and stammer. "You see, tomorrow's practice—um, I have to miss it."

The suspicion on her coach's face instantly transformed into disappointment and then, Kelley thought, into annoyance.

"And why is that?" Judi asked.

Kelley didn't want to lie, but Judi had actually given her the perfect excuse. She studied her coach's face, her steely eyes, and felt her resolve crumble. She knew Judi would question her love of gymnastics and the Bellevue Kips if she knew the real reason Kelley wanted to skip practice tomorrow and she just had to try the rhythmic. It was like a fire burning hot inside her. Judi wouldn't understand that. So, Kelley took a deep breath and lied.

"I have a physical therapy appointment tomorrow afternoon," she blurted out. "To check on my ankle. Make sure it's all healed up after last season."

All the annoyance and disappointment melted from her coach's face.

"Of course!" Judi said. "A good athlete has to listen to her body. You take care of yourself and we'll see you on Wednesday."

"Thank you, Judi," said Kelley. She felt the tension releasing from her body.

As she walked toward the changing room, Kelley felt a pang of shame for the lie. But then the realization that she was actually going to get to try rhythmic tomorrow washed over her and all regret melted away. She could feel the passion she felt for dance. And it felt wonderful!

How can that be wrong? she asked herself. And then she answered herself. *It's not!*

****

Kelley couldn't sit at all at school on Tuesday. During her last class, she was consumed with images of what her first Rhythmics class would be like. She'd packed her favorite leotard and warm-up gear in the purple gear bag she hadn't used since her dance days. It had been so long since she needed her ballet slippers and they had always made her feel so graceful and elegant whenever she wore them.

At last, the bell rang and Kelley raced for the front doors. Her mom was waiting for her in the Suburban, ready to get her right over to Edmond's Center for Rhythmic Gymnastics.

"Are you excited?" her mom asked as she pulled out of the parking lot.

Kelley looked at her and smiled. "Thank you for letting me do this, Mom. Thank you for understanding."

Her mom gave her a warm smile and turned her focus back to the road.

When they arrived at the Center, it took a little while to find the gym. From the outside, it was just a steel door at the back of an old warehouse with a small sign that read, The Rhythmic Gym. It wasn't as fancy as the Bellevue gym, but Kelley didn't need fancy.

She opened the door and her mom followed her into a surprisingly beautiful space. What looked like an old warehouse from the outside was actually a beautifully designed space inside. Kelley looked up to find huge skylights all across the very high ceiling. There were stained glass garage doors all along the far side of the room that Kelley imagined opened up to make the space even bigger. The different areas of the gym—the lobby, the front desk, the office, and waiting room—were all defined by walls with glass blocks randomly place within them. It made everything seem bright and happy. It looked like a brand-new, super modern and totally hip gym.

"Whoa," Kelley said under her breath.

"Impressive," her mom agreed.

"Kelley!" Cadence came running across the gym floor to greet Kelley. "I'm SO glad you could make it."

"Me, too!" Kelley laughed, still taking in the details of the space.

"My dad's an architect," Cadence explained to Kelley and her mom. "Just like my mom tests out all her choreography on me, dad tests out his design ideas on the gym. We're just one big experiment around here!"

"Welcome!" a warm voice came from behind them. Kelley spun around to see Cadence's mom, Gail, walking toward them. She hugged Kelley's mom and then Kelley. "We are so excited you want to give this a try!" she said to Kelley. Then she turned to her mom. "Cadence has been talking non-stop about Kelley for the last week!"

"I'll show you the locker room!" Cadence said, grabbing Kelley's arm.

"Have a great time!" her mom called out to her as she and Cadence headed toward the locker rooms.

As Kelley took in the whole of the gym, she was struck by how quiet and calm it seemed. With students on every piece of equipment all the time, Bellevue was always loud, no matter what time of day. She felt a new round of butterflies rise up. The quiet was intimidating.

But then Cadence opened the door to the locker room and everything changed. Kelley was overwhelmed by happy chatter. The energy inside the locker room was completely different from the gym floor. A dozen or so girls laughed and chatted and tossed hair bands to one another. They were obviously excited to be seeing each other after the long August break.

Kelley recognized a couple of the girls from the demo. The petite blonde with the long braid who'd done the ball routine was busy helping a smaller girl next to her. The girl who had done the amazing hoop routine ran up and hugged Cadence. For a minute, Kelley felt like a total outsider. She wanted to meet everybody, but she also wanted to hide in a corner.

How can I feel two such different emotions at the same time? she wondered. Is this what Jamie felt like when she walked into the Bellevue gym for the first time? *Mental note to tell Jamie what a rock star she is.*

"Don't be intimidated," Cadence whispered. "Everyone is really nice. Mostly. Come with me." She led her over to the blond-haired girl who was pulling the smaller girl's hair into a tight ponytail.

"Hey, Heather," she said. "This is Kelley, who I was telling you about. She's an *amazing* gymnast. We have to be *super* nice to her because we *definitely* want her to join our team!"

The older girls laughed as the little girl studied Kelley before launching into what seemed like an endless stream of words.

"Hi! I'm Raven. Are you really going to join our team? It's soooo much fun—especially the hoop. The hoop is my favorite. Your eyes are pretty. I have brown eyes like my daddy. Heather has blue eyes like my mom. Everyone says we don't look like we're sisters at all, but we are. I checked. We're not adopted."

Kelley burst out laughing as Heather put a hand over her sister's mouth to muffle her.

"Don't mind her," Heather said. "Raven likes to talk. *A lot.* But she's right. Rhythmics is fun. You're going to love it."

Cadence glanced up at the wall clock. "It's time! The coach's daughter has to be on time. And by 'on time,' I mean five minutes early."

The four girls walked out of the changing room together and headed over to the mats where four or five other girls were already warming up.

"Hey, there are a bunch of new girls tonight!" Heather noted. "Cool."

"That's a good thing," Raven said to Kelley. "So you won't be the only one. I'll hold your hand if you want."

"Thanks," said Kelley, taking the young girl's hand.

"We have to go help my mom," Cadence said. "You cool here by yourself?"

"And I have to take Raven over to the Cubbies Group," Heather announced.

"Will you be all right without me?" Raven asked Kelley.

"Absolutely," Kelley gave a smiling nod to all three girls. Then, she took her place with the other girls. There seemed to be about eight girls between 11 and 15 who all knew each other. The rest of the girls stood on the outside edges of the group. Kelley recognized their discomfort. She felt it in herself.

She was grateful when Gail suddenly appeared in front of the group, full of excited energy. She wore black Adidas athletic shorts and a bright pink running top. Her hair was pulled back into a loose braid, and just like at the lake, she didn't wear any makeup at all. She radiated a natural kind of warmth and exuberance.

"Welcome back, squad!" she said enthusiastically. It was clear she expected a response, but the gym went quiet. Gail furrowed her brow in fake disappointment. "I said *Welcome Back*, Rhythm Machine!!"

"Welcome back, Gail!" came back at her in shouts and giggles. Kelley could feel the nerves fall away just the littlest bit.

"We are going to have so much fun! If you're new, don't be nervous. We were all new once. Hardly anyone starts Rhythm Gymnastics with a whole lot of knowledge about what it really is. So whether your background is dance or gym, you will see a lot that is familiar in the skills. And you will see a lot that isn't familiar in the props! Just have fun with it. There's nobody here who didn't get totally confused and tangled in ribbon the first ten times they tried! But if you like it and you stick with it you will be amazed at what you will be able to do! Tonight we are just going to focus on basic skills and getting to know each other so we can all decide whether you are right for the team and whether the team is right for you! SO! If I can have my returning girls up front…"

Kelley watched the experienced girls line up along the front of the mat. The rest of the returning girls formed two lines behind them.

"We start every practice with a warm up," Gail said. "Extension is an important part of rhythmics and you don't want to do that without warming up! Go at your own pace, but try not to stop. All right, let's go! Kenna, lead the way!"

A slim, strong girl with alabaster skin and beautiful red hair sashayed to the front of the group before breaking into a jog and taking off around the perimeter of the gym. They all followed.

As Kelley fell in line, she couldn't help but continue to check out all the girls. Kenna reminded her of Bethany—a little bit impressed with herself. She also recognized two gymnasts from the Seattle Club where the Kips competed last year. Alexa with her short, strong build had been incredible on the beam at Nationals. Dawn was unnervingly thin, but she whipped around the parallel bars as if it was the easiest thing in the world.

Kelley was dying to ask them if they did both rhythm and artistic. Maybe they'd figured out how to balance both! Or maybe they were deciding on rhythmic over artistic just as she was thinking of doing.

After the third lap, Kenna led the girls back to the mats for floor work.

"Are you new too?" a quiet voice said from beside her on the mat. Kelley turned to see a girl looking at her with a warm smile and bright blue eyes.

Kelley smiled and nodded, not wanting to talk out of turn during warm ups.

"I'm Natascha," the girl whispered as she took a seat next to Kelley.

"Kelley," she whispered back. Kelley couldn't help but notice the girl's curvier, heavier build. She wondered if her build would make it hard for her to compete in rhythm gym. Then Kelley remembered her friend Emily who played goal on her soccer team. She had a very solid build and had been the best athlete on the team.

Up front, Gail took over for Kenna and led them through an intense series of crunches, pushups, planks, backbends, and handstands. Between each exercise, she called for a stretch. Kelley felt totally ready to go by the time Gail clapped her hands together and said, "Okay! Time for the fun stuff!

"We are going to take things step by step today," Gail said. "Every move builds on the move before it. Let's start with cartwheels. We do both sides for two-handed, one-handed and aerial, but don't worry about what you can't do. Just keep trying!"

The returning girls led the way as they all worked through the series. Kelley couldn't help but be impressed with the whole group. Everyone had clean cartwheels and aerials. She was in good company! It got tougher with the walkovers and not all the girls were able to do them one-handed on both sides but Kelley didn't miss a beat.

When Gail called out, "Back walkover into back chest roll into back tuck and layout!" Kelley flew through the sequence. She was feeling great!

"Okay, Everyone! Are you ready for a few props?"

An excited murmur ran through the girls as Gail brought out a collection of hoops.

They started with some very basic moves to get used to how it felt to move the hoop around leaping, reaching legs and arms. It was incredibly easy to get tripped up! The girls practiced swinging the hoop up and back, bending their knees into a slight plié as the hoop came down and back.

"Maintain straight arms on the swing," Gail instructed as she walked around with an eye on the new girls. Kelley was incredibly aware every time Gail seemed to be watching her. She wondered if she was looking as good as she felt.

The experienced girls demonstrated spinning the hoop from arm to arm, rolling it across the torso and spinning it on their head, neck, knees, and back. It was amazing! They could spin the hoop anywhere! Kelley tried every trick. Even though she nearly always dropped the hoop, it was a lot of fun to try.

Gail collected the hoops and introduced the clubs. Each girl was given a set of two and Kelley couldn't help laughing at herself as Gail led them through twirling and tossing.

This is going to take some time, thought Kelley, but she couldn't wait to try to ribbons and balls.

"The time flies by, doesn't it?" Gail said.

"Wait, what? It's over?" For the first time since class started, Kelley looked at the clock on the wall.

Cadence laughed. "We've been going for two hours!"

"Someone's a natural," Heather whispered as passed Kelley on her way to the locker room.

Kelley blushed but was bursting with joy. It had been so much fun, like she used to feel dancing. And to hear from someone as good as Heather that she was a "natural"? It couldn't get any better!

"Alexa? Natascha? Kelley? Would you come talk to me for a minute?"

Kelley headed over to talk to Gail, hoping against all hope that she was calling them over for a *good* reason.

"You each have wonderful skills and natural talent. It was a pleasure watching you today and I want you each to know that we would be thrilled to have all of you on our team."

Kelley felt a heat rise up in her face. She wanted to jump up and down and shout but Alexa and Natascha remained so calm and sweet that Kelley forced herself to do the same.

"I have to talk it over with my mom," Kelley said to Gail. She could hear her own excitement escaping in her high pitch. "But I just want you to know I had *such* a great time. Thank you so much!"

She wished she could stay at the gym and just keep practicing with her new friends, but she could see her mom waiting by the door. So she ran to the locker room and called out a good-bye to everyone before meeting up with her mom.

"So?" Kelley's mom's eyes shone just as brightly as her own.

"It was great! It was so much fun! Who knew I could hula hoop?"

"So are we about to make a seismic shift from Bellevue to Edmonds Center? Is this Rhythm over Competition?"

For the first time since she arrived at the gym, the reality of leaving the Kips settled in her stomach. At the same time, her phone buzzed with a new text message. She pulled the phone out and read the text. It was from Cadence.

You were gr8! Wanna join the team?

The high-flying elation of the afternoon was quickly disappearing. Kelley shut her phone off and put it back in her pocket.

She had no idea how to answer Cadence's question.

But she did know no matter what she decided, she was going to let someone down.

CHAPTER 4

"Aren't you forgetting something?" Kelley heard her mother's voice through a fog of exhaustion. She yawned as her mom placed the jar of mustard on the countertop in front of her.

"Thanks, Mom," she mumbled as she continued to struggle to make her lunch. It didn't matter that she was totally wrecked from hardly getting any sleep. There was a house rule that anyone old enough to have two numbers in their age was old enough to make their own lunch. In other words, where lunch was concerned, once you hit ten you were on your own.

Kelly had spent the night trying to stop her brain from running at warp speed as she wrestled with the question of artistic gymnastics or rhythmic gymnastics. Her thoughts had run in circles leaving her no closer than she'd been last night to knowing what she wanted to do.

She'd finally fallen asleep at four o'clock in the morning only to get trapped in a nightmare. In the nightmare, she was late for the Nationals competition because she couldn't find the arena and didn't know which leotard to wear. When she'd finally found the building, she circled it again and again just like the thoughts that circled in her head. She couldn't find the door and she kept trying to find anybody who could tell her which leotard she was supposed to wear. But all anyone would say to her was, "Black and fuchsia. Black and fuchsia. If you don't wear team colors, you'll make the team lose." Then she heard her name. It was loud and it kept repeating. Was it the announcer? Was it her turn

27

to compete?

That's when she awoke in a cold sweat and slowly realized her older brother was banging on her door, making sure she was awake and getting ready for school. Never had she woken feeling so completely exhausted.

"You look like you didn't sleep at all," her mom sounded worried as she packed some leftover kale salad for her own lunch.

Kelley leaned into her mom. It felt good to let her mom's arms close around her. She shut her eyes and for just a moment she allowed herself to feel safe the way she had when she was little—before life's questions got so hard to answer.

"Is it really that obvious?" Kelley asked.

"Well," her mom smiled, "you did almost put grape jelly on your bologna sandwich."

"Right," Kelley nodded. "I guess that's a giveaway."

"You want to talk about it?"

"It's just—" Kelley picked the rind off a slice of bologna. "I love gymnastics, but rhythmic feels more like... me...you know? I just—I don't know what to do."

Kelley's mom took the butter knife from her hands and gave her a warm kiss on the forehead.

"Why don't I finish up your lunch—just for this morning—while you get ready for school? Then, you might consider making a list of pros and cons. It's always helped me with complicated decisions. It's hard to choose between two great things. But it's a good problem to have. You're a talented girl, Kelley. I have absolute faith that you will excel no matter which activity you choose."

"Thanks, Mom!" Kelley gave her mom a quick hug before heading back upstairs to get ready.

On the bus, Kelley slipped into a front seat so she could focus on her Pros and Cons list undisturbed. She put her iPod to the classical playlist, a sure sign to her friends that she needed some alone time.

She pulled out her notebook and drew a big line down the center of page that divided it into two sections. Along the top she wrote GYM PROS over the first column and RHYTHMIC PROS over the second. Then she just stared at the near-blank paper.

She HATED making these kinds of decisions, having to decide between things she loved. It was dance and soccer and gymnastics all over again. It had been so hard to choose gymnastics over dance and soccer to be truly ready for State and Nationals last year. But she knew without a doubt that making that decision was what allowed her to do so well. She would have never placed so highly if she hadn't and she wouldn't trade that moment of victory for anything! Out of all the gymnasts at her level in the entire country, Kelley had placed sixth on beam. And she had only been able to do that because she'd been focused.

Plus, if she left now and didn't keep practicing all her gym skills, like vault and uneven bars, she was bound to lose them. Would that mean all that hard work was for nothing? Twelve years old seemed too young to have to make such huge decisions that could affect the whole rest of your life! *It isn't fair!*

Okay, she thought. *This isn't helping me.* Kelley took a deep breath to calm herself. *Inhale for six seconds, exhale for six seconds.* She forced her focus back to the words she'd written.

Two possibilities: Gym Pros, Rhythm Pros

Now, as her head continued to spin, she started writing down her thoughts in whichever box they belonged in.

Rhythmic combines so many of my interests. Rhythm PRO!

I could be a star of the most popular sport at the Olympics. Gym PRO!

I love being part of a team that works together like in soccer. Rhythm PRO!

Track record that includes some very nice medals. Gym PRO!

Beautiful costumes. Rhythm PRO!

Nationally respected team. Gym PRO!

Fewer Saturday practices—more soccer pick-up games. Rhythm PRO!

Get to see best friend every day. Gym PRO!

Fewer injuries in Rhythm than Gym. Rhythm PRO!

Judi thinks I look stronger and is excited about my future. Gym PRO!

Tumbling feels like flying. Gym PRO!
Dancing feels like floating. Rhythm PRO!
Everyone (almost) seems so nice. Rhythm PRO!
Everyone (almost) seems so nice. Gym PRO!
Wouldn't be the youngest. Rhythm PRO!
Would be the youngest. Gym PRO!
Brand new friends. Rhythm PRO!
Oldest best friends ever. Gym PRO!
I hate vault. Rhythm PRO!
I love tumbling and there's almost none in Rhythm. Gym PRO!

By the time Kelley's bus pulled up in front of her school, her page was filled with her lists but she still didn't have an answer. It all evened out. Ten positives for Rhythmic. Ten for Gym.

"Argh!" she couldn't help but say out loud. "What am I supposed to do?"

"Play soccer!" Her old soccer teammate and friend, Karen, was standing next to her waiting in line to get off the bus. "Everything's better when you play soccer at recess! You're looking like you need to clear your head. A goal or two might be just what you need!"

Teammates, Kelley thought. She loved how they knew each other so well and always knew just what to say.

"Good idea," Kelley said. "I'll see you on the playground at recess!"

****

Karen was right. Running around and focusing on the game kept her thoughts from spinning for a full forty minutes. But, as soon as the girls headed back into school, all Kelley's worries and lists of Pros and Cons came flooding back.

Kelley took a deep breath and headed to her Social Studies class even though she knew she'd never be able to concentrate.

She sat down just as the bell rang.

"Today we're going to do something a little different," Ms. G said.

Kelley exchanged looks with Karen who was sitting beside her. Ms. G had a habit of doing the unexpected every now and Ms. G also happened to be Kelley's old soccer coach. She was so cool, it was impossible to not like her class.

"We're going to watch a Martha Beck video. For those who don't know who Martha Beck is, she's Oprah Winfrey's life coach. As we think about the different ways people make decisions in their lives, it's interesting to hear what she has to say about following what your body tells you."

A quiet round of giggles circulated the classroom. Kelley just smiled. She knew by now that Ms. G liked hippy kind of stuff and Kelley respected Ms. G so she tried to stay focused. Besides, what were the odds that today she'd have a class dedicated to making decisions!? Weird!

As the video played, Kelley couldn't help but find it interesting. The way Martha Beck talked about listening to the subtle and not-so-subtle signs your body gives you about how it feels about something—it was really true. *Sure,* Kelley thought, *it may be hippie stuff, but a lot of it rings true.*

Kelley had listened to her body when she did gymnastics and was glad for it. It's why she'd started wearing grips to save her palms and wrists on the uneven bars even though some of the girls thought it was a sign of weakness. Kelley's body told her it needed the extra support. Her coach had also taught them to visualize themselves going through their routines step by step before competitions to work out any kinks. Could that same strategy help her make this kind of major decision?

That afternoon, as she rode the bus home, Kelley closed her eyes. She took a few short breaths and the noise of the other kids, the honking cars, the door opening and closing all faded. She built a picture in her head of herself with the Kips doing a workout. Then she just let the picture go and it came alive. She watched herself doing gymnastics. She felt all the movements as though she were in competition. The run-up to the vault, the small jump on the springboard, the twists she took in the air, she pictured all of it. She saw herself sticking her landing and smiling at the judges. Then she turned her attention to the way her body felt, from the top of her head to the tips of her toes. She noticed that her arms and legs felt tense and rigid. Her shoulders had risen, and her fingers and toes were crunched. Her stomach hurt. The familiar feeling of swirling butterflies was back and Kelley was only imagining a competition.

She opened her eyes and took another deep breath before closing them again. Then she started over, this time thinking about the rhythmic routine she had learned. Her body felt loose, fluid. She moved easily from one step to another. It was easy, natural. Every step felt completely within her comfort zone. She felt grounded and secure, like nothing could knock her over. Her arms felt light. Her feet felt balanced. There was never a hard landing. Kelley felt a smile appear on her face. Her shoulders relaxed. Her gut unclenched.

She opened her eyes and felt the sun on her face as the bus pulled up to her stop. *My body IS telling me something!* she thought. *It knows EXACTLY what it wants!* Kelley jumped up and nearly floated off the bus. The relief of having made the decision was extraordinary. As the bus pulled away, she pulled her cellphone out of her backpack. She typed a fast text to Cadence:

"Email me a list of practices. I'm in!!!!"

As she pressed SEND, Kelley turned her face to the sky to feel the sun. In that moment she knew that as good as it felt to have finally made the decision and as easy as it was to tell Cadence, it was going to be equally hard to tell her Kips family she was leaving.

But it was something she was just going to have to do.

CHAPTER 5

Thu-thump. Thu-thump. Thu-thump.

Kelley's heart was pounding hard as she walked toward the front door of the Bellevue gym. But there was no turning back. She had to tell Judi and she had to tell her squad.

Last year, when she'd had to tell Coach Judi she couldn't compete at the State finals because they coincided with her dance recital, she'd been in tears, but her mom had walked into the gym with her. This year, she was one year older and her mom had informed her this morning that this time, it was up to her.

"You made the decision," her mom had said during breakfast this morning, "so it's your job to talk it through with your coach and squad-mates."

Kelley knew she had one of the cool moms. She was fun, laughed easily, listened well, and treated Kelley like a grown-up. She was always involved in all the big decisions of Kelley's life, which she LOVED. But then there were these moments, when the other side of being treated like a grown-up wasn't so great. It would be such a relief right now to have her mom walking ahead of her, getting ready to break the news for her. Kelley loved being almost thirteen when it meant she could stay out later with her friends but not so much when it meant handling her own difficult conversations.

"Just get it over with, honey," her mom said as they pulled into the parking lot. "The anticipation is much worse than the reality."

33

"You sure about that?" Kelley said as she unhooked her seatbelt.

Her mom gave her a big hug.

"I'll wait for you in the car. You can do this."

"I can do this," Kelley repeated as she grabbed her fuchsia gym bag out of the back seat for the last time. "I can do this."

"Kell?"

"Yes?"

"You don't need the gym bag,"

"Oh, right," she murmured, truly grasping now that she was no longer a Kip. No more fuchsia and black. No more Kip, Kip, Hooray. Being a mature, responsible individual was kind of awful.

And then, Kelley was standing at the doors. She felt pretty sure she was going to pass out as she pulled open the door. The old familiar smell of sweat and talc and whatever that mystery element was that made the Bellevue gym smell like the Bellevue gym slammed her as she walked in. The smell brought on a wave of nostalgia and longing. She missed the gym already and she was still here.

Her eyes filled with tears as she knocked on the door of Judi's office.

The door swung open and Judi stood in front of her, a quizzical look on her face.

"What's wrong, Kelley?" Judi asked, getting up quickly from her seat.

"I need to talk to you," Kelley said. Then she took a deep breath, wiped her face with her sleeve, stepped into her coach's office and told her everything.

It was as if the lights went out as soon as she started talking. Because, as Kelley walked out of Judi's office, having told her she was quitting, she couldn't remember any of what had just happened. It was a blank. She knew she'd quit. She knew Judi understood but what exactly she said and how she felt and what Judi said—that was all a big blank.

But the relief Kelley felt as she left the office was extremely clear. She didn't feel any sense of loss for having just cut ties with gymnastics. Only the relief of having the news delivered rested gently on her head.

That must mean it was the right decision, thought Kelley. *Otherwise, it wouldn't feel so good.*

But then she was facing the locker room. She didn't expect she'd have the same feeling after telling her friends.

"Kelley!" Jamie ran up and hugged her the second she opened the door. "For a minute I was afraid you'd gotten injured again!" Jamie headed back to her things on the bench and continued getting ready as she talked and talked. "You better get your leo on. We're working on vault today and Nadia said that Raven is back from summer vacation with her dad so we're going to have a full squad today and—"

Jamie suddenly stopped mid-monologue. She looked Kelley up and down and took in her facial expression.

"Wait... where's your gym bag?" Jamie's voice sounded truly confused and maybe, Kelley thought, a tiny bit nervous about what she was about to hear.

Kelley's stomach seized. She felt her body locking down in all the places she'd felt when she did her visualization. Tension was building in every part of her body and she couldn't figure out how to speak. She couldn't think of what to say that would make this okay for Jamie. And saying something out loud was the only way she was going to release all this mounting stress.

"I quit," she finally blurted out. Silence. She repeated herself. "I quit."

"What?!" Jamie said, so shocked that it came out as a hoarse whisper. It was as if all the other noise fell away and everyone in the entire gym had heard her declaration. All the girls gathered around her.

"Whoa!" said somebody behind Kelley. She spun around and saw Nadia standing with a hand on her hip, refusing to be surprised. "Like we didn't see that one coming," she hissed.

"Nadia!" Jamie chastised.

"Well," said Nadia, "I just—I'm—" Nadia looked down to hide the single tear threatening to trickle down her cheek. "I'm sorry... " she whispered. "I wish you weren't leaving..."

"Wait... what?" asked Sara, always looking for clarification. "You're joining a different squad or you're giving up gymnastics completely?"

"I'm not going to be a Kip anymore," Kelley explained. She told them about joining the rhythmic squad. She wanted them to understand how it combined all her interests and had less of a risk for injury. Jamie's face softened. Sara moved closer. She leaned in so her arm pressed against Kelley's.

Kelley stopped talking and looked each one of them in the face. She was going to miss her Kips—her friends—so much.

"But I am still one of your best friends," Kelley added with determination even though everyone heard the waver in her voice.

"I still don't really get it," said Nadia, matter of factly. "After last spring, you were positioned to be one of the gym champions."

Nadia's comment quieted the room. Only Nadia was bold enough to break the silence she'd created. "Oh, well," she said as she grabbed a towel, "less competition for the rest of us, I suppose."

Kelley couldn't help but laugh. It was all so Nadia and, the truth was, beneath all her attitude, there was actually a very nice compliment in there about Kelley's skills as a gymnast!

With that, Nadia stuffed her gym bag into her locker and headed for the door. "You'll still come watch us compete, right?"

"Wouldn't miss it," Kelley said, smiling. Then she turned to Jamie and Sara, who both looked very uncomfortable.

Jamie was uncharacteristically quiet. Tears threated to spill out of her eyes at any second. But in typical Jamie fashion, she put a big smile on her face and said, "Well, I'll come over and help you train. You can teach me how to flick those ribbons."

"We'd better go or we'll be late," said Sara, not quite able to make eye contact. Kelley noticed Sara's nervous hand working the zipper of her hoodie, one of the things Sara did to soothe herself.

Jamie took Sara's hand. "We'd better go," Jamie said. "I'll text you." And the last two girls walked out of the locker room.

Kelley felt empty. Left behind. Like she was never going to see her friends again. As she walked out of the gym to the car, she wondered if she'd made the right decision. But then, the door opened behind her and Jamie came running out and grabbed her up in a huge hug from behind.

"You're going to be so AMAZING at rhythmics!" She gushed. "And we'll hang out every Sunday and text each other all the time, and...that must have been such a hard decision. I'm so proud of you."

Kelley turned around and gave her friend a big hug. Tears streamed out of her eyes.

"It was so hard," was all she could say. And, "I love you."

"I love you, too," said Jamie. "Now go kick some rhythmic butt. And I expect full details on your first day of practice.

"I promise," said Kelley.

The girls hugged one last time before Jamie ran back into the gym and Kelley climbed into the car where her mom was waiting with a reassuring smile on her face. Kelley pressed her head against the cool glass of the side window.

"I'm glad that's over," she said as her mom drove away from the gym.

But inside, she felt lost. As she watched the gym shrink in the side view mirror—it was as if all the hours, days, months and years that she had spent there were shrinking away too. As if her whole life was disappearing. It made it impossible not to wonder if she had made the right choice. But then she noticed something else in that rear view mirror. The smaller the gym and everything she knew became, the more open space was visible in the mirror. Suddenly, there was room for so much more!

Kelley took her eyes from the mirror and forced herself to look out the front. Look ahead! She told herself. Not behind. Because the future is unknown and so exciting!

CHAPTER 6

"Silly me," Kelley's mom said as she put away all the papers she'd just gotten from Gail during their first meeting. They were all walking out of Gail's office together. "I thought maybe your schedule would be a little lighter now that you're not competing in artistic gymnastics."

"Apparently not!" Kelley said, smiling. Her first practice was only moments away and she was a jumpy mix of excited and scared. But getting an overview from Gail had helped a little. Just filling out all the forms with her mom had made her feel a little calmer. Anything that helped her feel that she belonged here was welcome as far as Kelley was concerned!

Her mom had been so great last night, helping her feel better after the extremely hard day. She had found some amazing videos online of the 2014 European Rhythmic Gymnastics Championships. They'd made popcorn and climbed into her mom's big bed and watched it together. The commentary was hard to follow because it was in Spanish, but Kelley had a great eye for spotting mistakes and possible deductions. It was funny trying to figure out what the commentators were saying based on their tone of voice. One of the women gasped a lot whenever one of the girls in the group competition dropped a ball.

"Thanks for everything, Mom," Kelley said as she gave her a hug. "You really helped me a lot with getting to this point."

"I'm so proud of you," she whispered in Kelley's ear as she pulled a surprise Vitamin Water out of her bag and handed it to her. "Now go get rhythmic!"

Kelley strode into her first session as a rhythmic gymnast feeling as if she could do anything. Cadence and the other girls were already warming up. Soft music with a slow tempo was playing as the girls bent deeply into their stretches.

"Why don't you go join them?" Gail suggested from behind Kelley. "I'll be right over. I have a welcome surprise for you all today!"

Kelley nodded. She was excited but hesitant as she walked toward the other girls. They'd tried almost every piece of equipment the other day except ribbons.

Ribbons! They seemed so beautiful in the video last night, but looked as though they required a lot of mastery. The way the gymnasts could make them skim across the surface of the mat or swirl up into the air as if they were a string of fairies dancing on the wind. And it all seemed to happen with just a slight flick of the wrist. Kelley wondered if she could be so graceful.

"Kelley!" Cadence hooked her arm through Kelley's and escorted her over to the mats. "You remember Heather," she said, gesturing to the girl with the long braid.

"Hey!" said Heather with her ear pressed flat again the mat and directly next to her extended leg. "Glad you decided to come back. I guess we didn't scare you enough. We'll have to try harder next time." She gave her a huge warm smile. "Just kidding. Glad you decided to join the team."

Priya and Natascha both gave Kelley hugs. Natascha whispered, "We are going to have so much fun!"

Kelley noticed Alexa standing in the group.

"So you decided to join too?" Kelley asked.

"We're the newbies!" Alexa smiled at her.

Kenna, the infamous redhead, just stared at her as she sat calmly in a full split with her head resting on her bent elbows.

"Kenna?" said Cadence, "did you actually meet Kelley last time."

"I met her enough," Kenna said and then she dutifully nodded hello to Kelley before going back to ignoring her.

Cadence shook her head a little and gave Kelley a little nudge as if to say, don't worry about it! Kelley tried to let it roll off her back. This was training and Kenna was focused. She didn't want to be disturbed. Nothing wrong with that. In fact, it was even admirable!

"Okay, ladies,' Gail called as she plopped two gym bags full of equipment down next to the mat.

Kelley jumped in surprise. She hadn't heard Gail walk up.

"We are going to start with some basic skills across the floor. Who remembers our pivot sequence?"

Heather raised her hand and began to move through a series of pivots that went from a small move to a bigger move to a move where her leg was almost level with her hip as she turned on her standing foot.

"Great!" said Gail. "Let's move across the floor in that sequence. Remember, shoulders stay square and back straight! Heather and Cadence, lead two lines."

Kelley fell in line behind Cadence and easily worked through the pivot sequence.

"Hot shot!" Cadence whispered with a smile as they finished the sequence.

"Maybe you should lead the next one!" Natascha joked.

From there, Gail followed the same form with balance, leaps and flexibility. One of the girls would demonstrate a sequence and then everyone would move across the floor to practice the skill.

Kelley was even with Natascha as they hit balance poses between leaps across the floor. Kelley held them with ease for the five seconds that were required for each pose. She could feel Natascha wobbling even as she felt steady as a rock. On her other side, Alexa was doing pretty well with her first attempt too.

It almost felt like she was back in dance class. She had so loved the bar work and warm ups in ballet. But she also felt herself calling on many of her gymnastic skills—especially when it came to balance. She loved feeling that she was already good at so many of the steps.

The leaping sequence was quite simple and Kelley found herself wanting to take off and dance around the whole gym. But she stayed focused as she worked through each of the sequences as they were demonstrated.

"Excellent, girls!" Gail exclaimed as they finished up the warm up.

"Now it's time to make this really interesting.

"Finally," Kenna murmured, not loud enough for Gail to hear but plenty loud enough for Kelley's ears.

"We're going to do all the same moves but this time, you're going to toss and catch a ball throughout all of it!"

Kelley felt a twinge of nerves as she heard Kenna sigh in disgust. Clearly, Kenna wanted everyone to know how much the "newbies" were slowing her down. Kelley refused to look at her. She didn't want to risk letting Kenna psych her out. She was doing well and she wanted to stay on track.

She started moving across the floor in the pivot sequence while tossing the ball up in the air and trying to catch it. The first time the ball fell in front of her.

This is definitely harder with a prop! she thought. *This was so simple before. It's amazing what one little ball can do!*

Off to the side, Gail was calling out instructions. She tried to listen as she kept tossing the ball, dropping it, or catching it and then fumbling with her feet.

"Natascha, don't focus on catching. Watch Heather. She's making sure her arm is in the proper alignment as she moves it up and releases. She doesn't have to worry about catching, because if her release is perfect, the ball will be right where she expects it to be when she goes to catch it."

Kelley applied the direction Natascha had just been given to her own body. Suddenly, she was catching the ball and moving forward smoothly. A smile broke across her face. *There is nothing better than mastering a new skill,* she thought. *Balance Beam, Uneven Bars, and now Ball!* Kelley giggled softly to herself.

As they moved through the sequences, Kelley found that the ball made every move more difficult. But she also found that by listening to the instruction, no matter who it was directed to, she could improve quickly.

"Looking good, girls," said Gail after about half an hour of basic progressions. "Let's take a quick water break and then it's time for group choreo… with the ribbons!"

The girls broke into excited chatter.

"I'm a little rusty!" Natascha said to Cadence.

"What are you talking about? You look great!" Cadence told her.

Kelley hurried to fall in line with the two girls. She didn't want to get in Kenna's way, and aligning herself with Natascha and Cadence seemed like a good way to avoid that. But Kenna made it impossible to avoid her. She stood directly in Kelley's path just to make sure Kelley understood that Kenna had right of way. Kelley put her head down and stepped out of the redhead's way. She felt a spike of annoyance but it melted away when she felt Cadence's hand on her arm.

"Don't you feel more graceful already?" she asked and then, as if to prove her point, she leaped into a very impressive and highly dramatic grand jeté.

"Your extension is incredible," Kelley said.

"She's not human," Natascha said in a deadpan tone.

The girls laughed as they took the opportunity to rest for minute.

"Okay, girls," said Gail, "break's over!"

All the girls, even Kenna, jumped to their feet and hurried over to Gail. *This is a disciplined crew*, thought Kelley. She could feel the respect they all had for Gail and that reminded her again of her ballet classes. There was always the wonderful moment at the end of class when every dancer would line up to curtsy and thank the teacher. It always felt so elegant and civilized.

Gail continued, "This is the large group routine for demonstrations and possibly a half time performance for a Patriots game."

"Cool!" Natascha exclaimed so enthusiastically that it made everyone laugh.

"See?" Cadence whispered to Kelley, "we compete nationally too! AND we get to do cool performances in giant football stadiums. We're famous on SO many levels." She nudged Kelley's shoulder just like Jamie always did.

Kelley smiled and nodded. It was really cool! She'd never been to a live football game, but she had seen enough halftime shows to know she'd love to be in one. She pictured the squad flipping and dancing with ribbons as Beyoncé appeared in a puff of smoke in front of them singing her latest hit.

"You should also know," said Gail, "that I will be putting together a five-girl team in the next two weeks to compete at an elite level. So keep that in mind when you start thinking you might want to just mark the choreo instead of giving 110%!" She smiled but Kelley could tell she was serious at the same time. "Okay. Get your ribbons. If you don't have a ribbon, don't worry. I have extras."

Kelley approached Gail to get her ribbon and was a little stunned when she pulled a black and fuchsia ribbon out of her bag to hand to Kelley. What were the chances she'd get Kip's colors? That had to be a good sign!

"New girls, stand behind one of the experienced girls. Kelley, you can follow Cadence as we move through this choreo. Just so you can see how she holds the ribbon."

As Gail began to step through the opening sequence, Kelley immediately knew that the trouble would not be following the steps. They were quite simple. Jeté, jeté, turn to the left, relevé, plié, backbend, jump, jeté, jeté. It was a sequence she could do in her sleep. But keeping her extended arms and legs from getting tangled in the ribbon was another matter!

Not until the third time across the floor did she start to understand what Cadence was doing that she wasn't. It was the wrist. She had to extend her arms fully and work from the wrist.

As they waited for another run across the floor, Cadence leaned into her, "The harder moves are in the solos. Group is simpler because we have to be sooo synchronized!"

Kelley nodded. *It's plenty hard enough,* she thought. Besides, she loved the idea of working together on a piece like she had in ballet but doing gym moves at the same time. Simple or not, teamwork was so much fun!

Kelley stepped out to move across the floor again but this time stepped off-center and found her ribbon getting tangled with the girl in the next line over. She looked over quickly to apologize only to find Kenna glaring at her as she untangled the ribbon.

"Watch where you're going, newbie," she hissed. Then, before Kelley could even respond, Kenna was flashing a huge understanding smile in Gail's direction.

Wow, thought Kelley. *This girl just might be the Bethany of rhythmic gymnastics.* Kelley loved Bethany. They'd been friends forever, but once Bethany decided the reason she struggled on vault was because she was too tall she started taking her bad moods out on Kelley and Sara, who were both far more petite. Kelley remembered how hurt she'd felt that one of her closest friends resented her size. Not to mention all the horrible, snippy things Bethany had started saying. Practices had been miserable right before Bethany dropped out of Nationals.

Once the ribbons were untangled, Kelley stepped back in line and found herself next to Alexa who gave her a warm smile. The two of them took off across the floor and both executed the sequence almost perfectly.

"All right," called Gail, "moving on! Who has a clean thread-the-needle on the left side?"

Kelley's hand shot up before she even thought about it. So did Kenna's.

"Let's see Kelley," said Gail.

All at once, Kelley wished she hadn't raised her hand. She could feel Kenna's eyes burning holes into her back. But she knew she had to do her best because this was no time to not impress the coach. So without thinking about it anymore, she lifted her left leg and with remarkable grace and ease, moved it through her clasped hands until it was all the way through and perfectly extended before lowering it to the ground.

"Awesome!" Gail shouted. "So after the second set of double jetés, you will travel to center and take that position!"

Kelley couldn't believe she was already being put in a featured position. It would have been a completely wonderful moment if she hadn't felt a distinct chill as she passed Kenna on the way to center.

After practice, she packed up her bag quickly, hoping to avoid another run-in with Kenna.

"Hey!" said Cadence, plopping down next to her, "let's meet up at the lake this weekend. Are you going to be there?"

"I think so!" Kelley answered.

Just then, Kenna barged between them on her way to the door. Kelley looked at Cadence, feeling a little helpless.

Cadence spoke softly. "Don't worry about Kenna," she said. "She thinks she's queen of the gym and gets very touchy when she feels threatened. She'll work through it!"

Kelley nodded and pretended to "not worry about it."But as she headed toward the door, she couldn't help herself. She was officially worried about it. It was a little early in the season to already have an enemy!

CHAPTER 7

"Amazing, Mom! So amazing! I mean, it was terrifying too but in between those moments, it was ah-mazing! I really think this was the right choice. I mean, I absolutely feel sad about leaving my old friends and unfortunately, there's a mean girl at this gym too but still... Mom! AH-mazing!"

Kelley couldn't stop talking. She felt so excited and happy and anxious, all at the same time. It felt like talking was the only thing that would keep her from exploding. So it wasn't until they were sitting in their driveway that Kelley realized her mom had been almost completely quiet all the way home.

"Everything okay, Mom?" she said as they walked toward the door.

"You were so happy when you got in the car, I just thought we could wait until we were home to talk."

Kelley's stomach dropped. What was so wrong that her mom would put off talking to her about it?

"What?" Kelley asked as she set down her bags on the counter.

Her mom sat down at the kitchen table in front of a bunch of papers. Her laptop was already open as if she'd been working right before she left to pick Kelley up from the gym.

"I got home from dropping you off and started going through the paperwork Gail gave us and, well... the financial commitment has caught me slightly off guard."

Kelley thought her stomach had already taken a hit, but she felt that same horrible dropping feeling again as she realized where her mom's words were headed. She was going to have to quit before she'd even begun. She felt frozen in her seat.

Her mom went on, staring at the computer screen. "In addition to the cost of lessons, which I had thought about, there are also new uniforms which are surprisingly expensive... and a new team costume and warm-up suit that is also remarkably expensive. And then, there's the equipment." Her mom was rubbing her temples the way she did when she was struggling to figure something out.

"I guess I thought we just used the equipment that was at the gym," Kelley said.

"I did, too," her mother nodded, "but apparently not. There is actually a fee for equipment usage that I had not anticipated." Kelley mother was silent for a full minute, just thinking.

"I hadn't budgeted for that much possible additional expense when we talked about switching," she finally said.

Her mom's face looked sad. It made it impossible for Kelley to be mad at her. But it didn't stop her from feeling mad at the situation and to dread having to tell her new friends and coach that she wasn't going to be able to be on the team after all. And she also felt plain old sad at the idea of not being able to feel like she felt today regularly.

Tears welled up in Kelley's eyes. She bit at the nail on her left thumb, like she used to do when she was little.

"Mom," she started, "let me just—"

"We're going to have to make some sacrifices," her mom said as if Kelley hadn't just started to speak.

Kelley's head spun a little bit. *Wait*, she thought, *what? Sacrifices?*

"You mean I don't have to quit?" Kelley sputtered.

"No, of course not," her mom said, still very seriously, "You made a commitment to the team. But you do have to sit here and help me figure out where we can come up with the extra money each month."

Kelley jumped to her feet. "I can do that! I can absolutely do that!" The relief in that moment was so complete she felt as though she was floating. "For starters, she said, don't even think about the costumes right now. I will search eBay and I'll talk to the other girls—there has to be a way to get good used ones."

"Okay," her mom said as she started pecking at the keyboard of her laptop. "That would help a lot if you could do that. But we're still left with $675 more in expenses than I budgeted for."

"So what does that come to every month?" Kelley asked.

"It's a little more than $70 a month if Gail will let us pay over the whole year. If the training wasn't already so expensive this wouldn't be such a big deal. But you know how much we have already done to figure out covering that expense."

"Mom, I totally get it and I do know how much you've done to make all my training possible and I don't take it for granted." She wished she was old enough to work. If she could, she would get a job and cover all the expenses herself.

"So any ideas on where we can cut back?" her mom asked.

Kelley thought about where she spent most of her allowance. She already packed her own lunch—cafeteria food wasn't even made out of real ingredients, super-gross—except for pizza day, so she could cut that out. She thought about how much she loved her morning hot chocolate and bran muffin at Starbucks. And then she thought, *not nearly as much as Rhythmic.*

"I could give up Starbucks," Kelley suggested.

"Wow," her mom smiled. "You really do want to do this, don't you?"

"And," Kelley said, too busy thinking to respond to her mom's ribbing, "we talked about buying costumes on eBay, but what about selling some? We have a ton of old ballet and gymnastics costumes and leos and a lot of them are in great shape—" Kelley felt a twinge of sadness at her own suggestion. There were so many memories in those outfits. The first time she tumbled. Her first routine at Optionals. She always assumed she'd have them forever to show her own kids someday. But staying on the Rhythmic team felt even more important.

Before long, they agreed that they had a good plan in place. Kelley headed upstairs feeling really good—not just about her day at the gym but about being able to work out the financial end with her mom. It felt as though she was really stepping up and taking responsibility for her own training.

After her shower, she lay on her bed watching YouTube clips from the 2014 World Rhythmic Championships. She was texting with Cadence who was watching the same thing on her bed at her house. Kelley had a million questions about every routine. She wanted to know everything she could about Rhythm. But she also just liked going back and forth with Cadence about the beautiful costumes and the amazing performances. She was also responding to texts and posts from all her other new teammates, all of whom were adding her to their contacts lists for Instagram, Snapchat, and Facebook.

"So costumes," Kelley texted Cadence. "Where to find good used ones?"

"Have million old costumes U can rework for yr solo," Cadence texted back. "Will bring to lake this weekend."

Kelley smiled. It was all going to work out. She could feel it. She returned to the videos, admiring the extension of the gymnasts and the absolute precision of the team choreo. She found herself admiring Yana Kudryavtseva of Russia who won the competition. She didn't have to give up her dreams of winning Olympic gold or hearing the US national anthem play as she stood on the podium just because she'd no longer be performing on the balance beam.

When Kelley had gone through every video she could find that featured Yana Kudryavtseva, she went to the Gymnastics USA website to see how group and individual competition worked in rhythmic gymnastics.

In the individual all-around, each athlete competes in four out of five events, hoop, ball, clubs, ribbon, and rope. The athlete's final score is the sum total of all the events added together. So even if you are good at ribbon, you could lose standing by dropping a club. That felt pretty familiar to Kelley since it wasn't too different from artistic gymnastics.

The big difference was the group competition. In artistic gymnastics, each individual athlete's scores were added together with teammates' scores to come up with a group score for the team. So there was a team score but it was all based on solo performances. Teammates were never on the mat at the same time. In rhythmic, five gymnasts compete in two different routines. In one of them, all the gymnasts use the same prop. In the other, the gymnasts use two different props—like three would use the ball, and two would use the hoop.

Kelley thought that one sounded really fun... and really hard! She giggled imagining ribbons tangled in hoops colliding with clubs. A mess! She continued reading.

One score was given for each group routine and then the two scores were combined for a total score in the "group all-around."

Ding! Another message. Kelley saw Nataschsa's favorite emoticon pop up, a cartwheeling smiley face.

"You rocked it today!" appeared on her screen.

Before Kelley could respond, her phone dinged again and she saw Jamie's name.

"SO????!!" the first message said. Then, "Deets, pls!!"

She'd promised Jamie she'd give her all the details of her first day's practice, but she'd been totally caught off guard by her mom's money conversation. And the messages just kept coming.

There was a Snapchat image of Kelley with the ribbon, taken at practice today. Across the picture were the words, "Great arms!"

Then there was an instant message from Cadence, "Found perfect costume for u! U will luv!"

An hour later, Kelley finally shut her laptop and crawled into bed, excited to dream about swirling ribbons, bouncing balls, and spinning hula hoops. Then she remembered Jamie. She pulled out her phone to text her back just as her mom walked in.

"No more cell, Kelley,"

"But I promised—"

"It can wait until tomorrow." She waited for Kelley to turn off her phone and then she took it and put it in a drawer before kissing her good night.

I cannot forget to call Jamie in the morning, Kelley chanted to herself. *Call Jamie. Call Jamie.*

She tried to keep the chant going in her head as she drifted off to sleep. But images of beautiful ribbons and shiny balls and of herself floating through the air like a ballerina kept intruding on thoughts of her old friend.

CHAPTER 8

Kelley stood in Cadence's bedroom at the lake feeling as though she had won a shopping spree. Countless gorgeous old costumes were laid out on Cadence's bed and Kelley got to try on every one of them.

"Try on the green one!" Cadence said. "It'll look so good with your eyes."

But Kelley was holding up another costume. "There's no material here!" she laughed. "Your mom let you wear this?"

"I was six! That was all the material I needed when I was that little! I just pulled it out in case you were handy with the sewing machine. That sequin appliqué is so pretty. It could be taken off and put on something else." Cadence pulled another costume from the pile. It was a blue-green leo with only one long sleeve. On the other arm was a collage of gold, red, and green fabric that looked like feathers around the wrist. A short skirt covered in a feather pattern was stitched to the bottom.

"Try this one," Cadence insisted. "It's one of my favorites. I wore it the very first time I won a gold medal for clubs!"

"But I might look like a parrot," Kelley giggled.

"Okaaay," said Cadence as she dug deeper into the pile. She pulled up another costume. "How about pinkish-purple?" she asked.

"It's actually fuchsia," Kelley said as she felt a tinge of longing for her old Kips' fuchsia and black combination. "It's pretty but maybe not for me." *This is a fresh start*, she thought. *I need new colors.*

Kelley pulled out a simple long-sleeved, deep red leotard. It had sequins that spiraled from front to back and an asymmetrical V-neck that dipped down on the left side and led into a sparkly silver and lavender stripe. There was a smattering of sequins on the sleeves as well. It seemed basic, but it was elegant and the back was truly unique. The leotard looked almost as if it was backless except for the diagonal stripe of sequins where the swirl wound around from the front. It was stunning from all sides!

Kelley held it up to herself and looked in the mirror. "I think this may be the one." She quickly stepped behind Cadence's closet door and pulled off her jeans so she could try on the costume. "Are you ready for this?" she asked before stepping out to show Cadence her new look.

"Ooh!" cooed Cadence. "It's perfect!"

"It feels so grown up. Or at least teenager-y," Kelley said. She couldn't keep a smile from her face.

Cadence laughed. "You'll drive the boys insane!"

Kelley blushed and looked away as she suddenly pictured a particularly cute boy from her Social Studies class. He had shared his textbook with her last week when she'd left hers in her locker and she couldn't help but imagine what he might think if he saw her perform in this costume.

"Wow!" smiled Cadence. "Who are you thinking about?!"

"No, no, no," denied Kelley and then she quickly changed the subject. "Will you take my picture in this? I want to send it to Jamie to see what she thinks."

Cadence carefully framed the shot and then snapped it. But when Kelley tried to send it to Jamie, she couldn't get a strong enough signal. The message failed.

"I'll do it later," she said. Then she turned back to the mirror.

"Thank you so much for letting me wear one of your costumes," she said to Cadence. "You have no idea how much you're helping me."

"No. I think I do. That leotard you chose was $450 new! Rhythmics is an expensive sport!"

Kelley felt that old familiar churning in her stomach. $450? How could anybody afford that? Had her mother figured on that much when she calculated the expense the other night?

"Do you think the team costume is going to cost that much too?" asked Kelley.

"I don't know, but I do know my mom tries to keep the cost down when she can. The only reason I got that one was because she got it at a serious discount when she was buying so many other things for the rest of the girls at the same time."

Kelley nodded nervously. She found herself wondering if it was wrong to start hoping NOT to be picked for the elite group. That would make things at least a little bit more affordable. But then in the next moment she thought how much she *really* wanted to be selected for the elite team.

"Don't worry," Cadence could see she was concerned. "I know my mom will figure out a way to make it work for everybody."

Her smile was so warm and sincere that Kelley couldn't help but feel better. *Everything's worked out so far,* she thought. *No reason to think it won't keep working out!*

She sat down on Cadence's bed. It was a cozy room, small but so comfortable. Every inch was covered in something to do with gymnastics or dance.

"Is your room at home like this too?" Kelley asked.

"Pretty much," nodded Cadence. "There's really nothing else that makes me as happy!"

"I know how you feel!" Kelley nodded. "It's the best!"

The weekend flew by. It was an almost-summer kind of warm. The girls were able to forget for a moment that it was fall and that, with their schedules, this was probably the last weekend at the lake until the spring. They swam and rode their bikes and even got to kayak across the lake. Conversation was endless with gossip about everything from bad behavior at the gym to what was happening with 5 SOS. But there were two topics that just kept coming up no matter what else was being discussed—the elite team and Donovan, the extremely cute boy who was visiting Cadence's neighbors.

"So! Who do you think is going to be on the elite team?" Cadence asked as they sat on the beach and admired Donovan as he expertly tied up the rowboat he'd just returned to the dock.

"We've been through this!" Kelley laughed. "I told you I don't know everyone well enough to say but I really, *really* hope I'm one of them."

"I know," said Cadence, laying back and kicking her legs up over her head. "I do too. And I hope I'm standing next to you!"

"Would you like to discuss whether Donovan thinks we're cute again too?" Kelley teased as she continued to watch the boy.

"I absolutely would! Thanks for reminding me!"

"So?" Kelley pushed her to say something.

Cadence sat up, looked down to the water and then fell back again, giggling. "No! Nothing! I really don't want a boyfriend. I think it's silly at our age, to tell you the truth... even if it is funny to watch my friends act like idiots around them."

"Agreed!" Kelley nodded. "Besides, I am way too busy to add a boyfriend into my schedule."

"Exactly," said Cadence, sitting up again to take another look at Donovan. "He is SO cute, though."

"Yeah," said Kelley as she secretly snapped his picture from afar, "he really is."

She tried again to Snapchat Jamie. Kelley was sure Jamie would think Donovan was extremely good-looking too. She tried to send the photo three times but it failed every time. A wave of guilt ran through her as she realized she and Cadence were sitting in exactly the same place she and Jamie had been sitting just before they met Cadence.

I hope Jamie doesn't think I'm replacing her, thought Kelley. *Best friends forever!* And she hoped Jamie was thinking the same thing.

CHAPTER 9

The gym was buzzing with a quiet focus as all the girls worked on their individual skills. Kenna was practicing a complicated club catch that included a double pirouette between the toss and catch. Natascha was focused on her stretching. She had incredible extension with an over-split on both sides. It was amazing to watch her foot go beyond the top of her head when she kicked up! But even so, Natascha was always trying to improve.

Cadence was running through her ball routine. Kelley couldn't help but stop and watch her. She was so good with the ball. But then again, Cadence was really good with all the equipment.

Her lifelong obsession has really paid off, thought Kelley, as she watched Cadence toss the ball before falling into a front roll that continued into a backbend, at which point Cadence extended her leg straight up as the shiny red ball landed exactly perfectly on the bottom of her upturned foot.

"Wow!" Kelley whispered to herself as she turned back to the hoop and the mat where she was working on a pirouette into grand jeté move that included a hoop toss and catch. This was her favorite of all the moves she'd learned so far. Her fingers wrapped lightly but securely around the hoop as she prepared for her first pirouette.

It was Wednesday and the week was racing by. Every day was packed with school, homework, and gym practice. But as Kelley was getting ready to come to the gym this afternoon, she felt a new wave of confidence. She realized this was the first day she would arrive at the gym having at least *tried* each piece of equipment.

She'd done ribbon and ball last week. On Monday, Gail had brought out the hoops. On Tuesday, she'd gotten a chance to work with clubs and then, they practiced some rope skills.

Without a doubt, Kelley's favorite piece of equipment, or *apparatus* as the Kips used to say, was the hoop. She just loved the way it felt as she sent it spinning in the air only to have it land back so gently in her hand after she'd completed a skill like a leap or a grand extension. She felt as though she was in perfect unison with the hoop. That was not exactly true about the clubs or the rope. She just didn't have the same sense of timing. It was harder to figure out exactly when they'd be coming back down in her grasp. But she wasn't upset about those skills coming a little more slowly. Overall, she knew she was doing really well for her second week!

She threw the hoop up into the air for her third consecutive jeté. Then she reached all the way through her fingertips and like magic, the hoop fell directly into the palm of her hand.

"You seem to have a very natural feel for the hoop!" Gail said as she approached Kelley.

"I love it!" Kelley gushed. "It's so much fun!"

"Well, then," Gail nodded. "That's where we'll start with your choreo. But just remember, you have to have four routines with four different pieces of equipment to compete. And we don't have a lot of time. So keep working with the clubs and ribbon!"

"I know," nodded Kelley. "I was just about to switch."

"Hoop is really the easiest," Kenna said just loud enough for the girls to hear but not Gail. She tossed a club into the air and did a double pirouette before catching the club perfectly. Then she said, "Clubs are definitely the hardest."

Cadence laughed, "Whatever, Kenna! They're all challenging." She turned to Kelley and winked. "Wanna take a break?" she asked her.

Kelley nodded. She grabbed her water bottle and headed over to the stack of mats that ran along the wall. Cadence motioned to Natascha to join them. Kelley could feel Kenna's eyes on them. It seemed impossible she would actually be waiting to be invited to join them too after being so mean but regardless, that was how it felt. The three girls sat close to each other and each of them avoided Kenna's eye.

"Only one more week!" Cadence said with a note of suspense in her voice.

She was talking about her mom's announcement. By next week at this time, they would know who would be competing on the elite team.

Kelley watched Alexa working with the ball. She looked really strong. So did the girls who were over by the waiting area doing a ribbon twist in unison. And, even though Kelley hated when mean girls were actually good at things, Kenna was really, *really* good. She was amazing the way she never missed a club catch. Kelley knew half of them wouldn't make the team and she wondered if she would be in that half.

"Well," said Natascha, "I've always looked especially attractive sitting on the bench."

The girls laughed quietly. Kenna glared at them as if she were certain they were laughing at her.

"You both are totally in the running," Cadence said to Kelley and Natascha.

"Only if it's 100% hoops!" Kelley smiled.

"Or at least absolutely no clubs! I don't want to say Kenna's right," whispered Natascha, "but they are really hard!"

Kenna face grew red as she watched the girls whisper and giggle. It was clear they were talking about clubs so they must be talking about her.

"I think they're all hard in different ways," Cadence said to Natascha.

Kelley was just about to agree when—*WHIZ!*—something flew past her ear and directly into Natascha's face. In a split second, the room went from a quiet focus to crashing chaos and in the middle of it, Natascha was holding her face in her hands as blood streamed from her nose.

Kelley's head whipped around to figure out where the flying object had come from. Kenna was standing on the mat holding only one club. Kelley looked back at Natascha who was shouting and crying. Kenna's other club was resting on the ground at Natascha's feet.

"My nose!" cried Natascha. "My nose!"

Gail came running toward them as Cadence turned on Kenna.

"What did you do?!" Cadence shouted at Kenna. "It was an accident!" she insisted. "It slipped!"

"It looks broken," Gail said. "We need to call your parents and get you to the hospital.

Kelley looked at Kenna in disbelief.

"What are you staring at?" Kenna demanded. "I said it was an accident. Like I would really throw a club at someone!"

Kelley looked away. She didn't want to say anything she'd regret. Besides, right at this moment, Natascha needed her.

****

It wasn't until the next morning that Kelley got a text from Natascha letting her know that she was okay.

"Don't look so pretty," her text read, "but u will luv my new nose guard! C u at practice!"

Kelley couldn't believe Natascha was going to be at practice. *She is one tough gymnast,* thought Kelley. She wondered if she'd have the stamina and strength to show up the next day after getting her nose broken by a bully. She wasn't sure.

When Kelley got to the gym after school, Natascha was already there. Kelley gasped a little when she saw her. Natascha wasn't kidding about how she looked. Kelley was shocked at how black and blue her face was. Natascha had two black eyes.

"It's not as painful as it looks," Natascha laughed as all the girls gathered around her.

Kelley looked around for Kenna. She couldn't imagine what she must be feeling. If Kelley had done something like that to another person she would be devastated. But Kenna slipped into the locker room without even saying hello to Natascha.

"We're going to start with the group piece today," Gail announced.

"We are so glad you're here today, Natascha. But just so everyone knows, Natascha is going to observe for the next couple of days and mark some of the choreography before she really gets back into the action!"

Everybody burst into applause and Natascha blushed a little.

"Before we get going, I have an exciting drawing to show you all. This will be our team leo."Gail held up a sketch of a leotard in a beautiful lavender. Kelley loved the color but as she studied it, she was a little worried about how revealing it was. The leotard was very sheer over the shoulders and Kelley was pretty sure that would make it hard to wear a bra. She tried to judge the other girls' reactions, but she couldn't tell what they were thinking.

"Okay!" Gail clapped her hands and all the girls found their positions. They ran through the opening steps they'd learned last week and earlier this week and then Gail dived into brand new choreo. Kelley was amazed at how smoothly it went.

These girls are really good, Kelley thought. She was amazed to look at the clock and realize that practice was almost over. They had gotten almost halfway through the routine already and every girl knew what she was doing.

"It's going to be tough to get onto the elite team," Kelley whispered to Cadence on the way to the locker room. "Everybody is soooo good!"

As Kelley and Cadence packed their bags, Natascha slipped into the locker room and sat near them.

"What's wrong?" Cadence asked. "Are you in a lot of pain?"

"It's not that," Natascha said quietly and then looked around to make sure no one was near. "It's that leotard. I'm really not comfortable with it. There's no way we're going to be able to wear a bra with it. It just looks really revealing, you know?"

Kelley felt bad for Natascha. She'd been so impressed with her that she'd stopped noticing that she was a little curvier than the rest of them.

"Just because it won't look good on your body doesn't mean you should ruin it for the rest of us," came a nasty hissing voice from around the corner of the lockers.

Kelley gasped as they all turned to see Kenna standing there.

"Haven't you done enough damage!?" Cadence hissed back at her.

"It's an awesome costume," Kenna said. "And if she doesn't want to wear it then she should drop out."Kenna turned on her heels and disappeared out the door.

Kelley and Cadence were left with a sobbing Natascha.

"She is sooo mean!" Natascha cried. "And I have to stop crying because I cannot get a stuffy nose at this point!"

"I'm going to talk to my mom," Cadence announced. "This has gone too far! She's nothing more than a bully!"

Moments later, Cadence returned to the locker room with her mother beside her.

"I'm sorry, Natascha," Gail said. "Cadence told me what Kenna said. I will talk to her, you can be sure of that!"

Kelley could tell Gail was not happy about the situation. Just then, her phone buzzed with a new text message.

"You girls get home now," Gail said. "And Natascha, don't worry about this. We'll straighten this out. You just get some rest."

As Kelley headed to the car, she opened the text.

Jamie! Ugh! How could she have forgotten to message her again?

"KELLEY!!!!!!!" the text read. "Did you get eaten by a hoop? The Kips miss u. Snapchat so we know u r alive!"

"Sorry!" Kelley quickly typed. "Still love you best, Bestie!"

She waited for her phone to buzz again all the way home. But there was no response.

Jamie must have gone into practice right after sending that text, she thought. I'll have to call her after I get my homework done.

Staying in touch with her best friend without the Kips was already harder than Kelley had thought it would be.

CHAPTER 10

"Hi, Mom!" Kelley chirped as she piled into the front seat of the Suburban.

"Welcome to Friday afternoon!" her mom smiled.

"Thank you," Kelley laughed. "It's a pleasure to be here!"

"Your gear is in the back seat," her mom said as she put the car into gear and headed toward the gym. "And I packed an extra-special snack for you today."

"Chocolate chip cookies?"

"Maybe. I can't reveal my secrets."

Kelley rested her head against the backrest and closed her eyes. She was excited to get to practice and she wanted to be focused when she got there. She closed her eyes and started visualizing her hoop routine just the way she'd learned to do watching the Gail video in her social studies class. Kelley knew she still had a ton of work to do to really master the hoop, but she also knew she had a natural ability with it. It was as if all her balance and timing that had been so important in dance, soccer, and artistic gymnastics were exactly what made someone good at hoop.

She saw herself walking to the center of the mat. She even imagined herself wearing the beautiful costume she was borrowing from Cadence. Gail had given her mom full permission to do whatever she needed to make the costume fit Kelley perfectly and so her mom was altering the hem a little to really highlight the line of Kelley's very long legs.

Kelley focused hard and saw herself setting the hoop down over the top of her left foot with her right foot just outside the hoop. Her arms were precise as she put them behind her back and clasped them together. Then she began to hear the music, and she visualized herself beginning her routine. Her right foot lifted up and stepped behind her left foot to the far side of the hoop so she could give the hoop a quick kick to get it spinning around her left ankle. Then she stepped back over the spinning hoop and pulled the hoop around so she could lay it on top of her right foot.

This is where it got really exciting. In a fast move, she lifted her right leg with the hoop hooked around her foot while lowering her head so her leg fully extended up toward the ceiling and sent the hoop straight up in the air. While it sailed up and back, Kelley windmilled her body in a perfectly timed move so her hand was reaching up and back just as the hoop fell back toward the ground. Then she grabbed the hoop in front of her with both hands, like the steering wheel of a car, and threw it high into the air as she headed into two complete airborne spins. She landed with a forward roll that allowed her to extend her leg up just as the hoop fell toward her. She was so perfectly positioned the hoop came down directly over her leg, and she was able to rotate her leg at the same time so the hoop was grabbed by her bent foot and began spinning around her ankle.

"How's it going?" her mother asked, interrupting her visualization. "You falling asleep over there?"

"I just saw myself doing a perfect opening to my hoop routine!"

"Oops," her mom said, "sorry to interrupt!"

"I love the hoop! Absolutely love it!"

"Well, I can't wait until parents are allowed to watch!"

Kelley gazed out the window and smiled. Things were really feeling good. Training was great, but it also felt as if other things were starting to work out too. She'd finally remembered to call Jamie and they had made a plan to meet at the mall this Saturday after they were both done with their practices.

They had spent some key bonding moments at the mall. They called it "Retail Therapy," even though they rarely bought anything. Kelley had always chosen not to buy stuff, because she knew Jamie's mom didn't have much extra spending money and she didn't want Jamie to feel left out. Now, with the added expenses Kelley and her mom were trying so hard to cover, Kelley was grateful that spending money was never an important part of hanging out with Jamie. But that didn't mean they couldn't meet at Starbucks and start their day with a little mocha-flavored splurge! It would be really nice to reconnect with Jamie. There was so much to tell her!

Just as Kelley was reaching for her gear bag in the back seat, her phone buzzed.

It was a text from Cadence.

Kelley gasped. "Mom," she said, grabbing her mother's arm dramatically

"What is it, honey?" her mom asked. "Is everything okay?"

"Practice is off," Kelley said.

"What do you mean, practice is off?" her mom pulled the car to the side of the road.

"I don't know. It's a text from Cadence and it just says practice is off and she will fill me in later."

Her mom looked out the window as Kelley stared at her mom. It was as if they suddenly had no idea what to do now they weren't racing to get somewhere on time.

"I guess we have a night off!" her mom laughed.

"I know!" Kelley said with a smile. "What do people do with nights off?"

"I'm not sure... but I hear sometimes they actually sit down, put their feet up, eat popcorn and watch movies."

"Movie Night!" Kelley exclaimed, overjoyed at the notion of spending the evening in one of her favorite ways. Suddenly, a cancelled practice seemed like a pretty good idea.

Kelley and her mom stopped at a convenience store on the way home and loaded up on new nail polish colors, glitter, popcorn, chips, guacamole, salsa, chocolate donuts, ice cream, and milk—everything they would need to have the most awesome movie night in the history of mother-daughter bonding.

"Grab a deck of cards, too," her mom said. "It's about time I taught you how to play Rummy. Did you know it's a family tradition?"

Kelley looked at her mom quizzically.

"My mother taught me to play and her mother before her. Every Monday night when I was a kid, my grandmother and her two sisters would come over and play Rummy with my mom in the kitchen while my Great Uncle sat in the living room with my dad watching football."

"That's really cool," Kelley said, as she steered her mom toward the soda aisle. "And what were you doing while they played?"

Kelley's mom got a faraway look on her face as if she were picturing the scene. "When I was really little, I sat under the table listening to their stories. When I got older they let me play, too."

"And did you win?" Kelley asked as she snuck a liter of Coke into their cart.

Her mom winked. "I can't reveal my secrets."

****

"I can't wait to hear why practice was cancelled," Kelley said as she and her mom headed toward the gym the next afternoon. She held her fingers up to the light and admired the flags her mom had painted on her nails the night before—one for each of the top ten countries in rhythmic gymnastics. Kelley's mom had been right. Mani-pedis, movies, junk food, and cards had been the perfect way to spend her night off. Kelley felt refreshed and ready to give the ribbons a twirl.

"You didn't hear anything else from Cadence?" her mom asked as they pulled into the parking lot.

Kelley didn't answer her. She was looking at the gym door and trying to figure out why Gail, Cadence, several other girls, and their parents were standing outside.

"That looks suspicious," her mom said.

They got out of the car and walked toward the group standing around Gail. They could hear Gail explaining the situation to the rest of the parents.

"If everyone could gather around so you can all hear," she said.

Kelley and her mom crowded in with everyone else.

"It seems someone reported our building as being a fire hazard and unsafe for children," she said.

Kelley could sense concern rising up among the adults. The girls began to whisper to each other.

Fire hazard? Kelley thought. *Everything is brand new.*

"I assure you this is a misunderstanding and we will have it resolved as soon as possible. The Fire Chief has scheduled a full inspection for next week and in the meantime, we cannot use the gym."

Kelley felt a tug on her arm. She turned to see Cadence gesturing to her and Heather to come stand by her. As Gail continued to talk to the parents, the two girls leaned in toward Cadence as she whispered to them.

"Wait till you hear the *real* story! After practice on Thursday—" Cadence glanced at Kelley. "*You* remember Thursday and how charming Kenna was being?"

Kelley nodded.

"Well, I was waiting for my mom after practice and I overheard her talking to Kenna's mom about everything. She told her mom that Kenna was really bullying one girl in particular and she couldn't allow that behavior to continue in the gym."

"What did her mom say?" Heather whispered.

"Well, my mom said she wanted to put Kenna on probation for a period of time so she might really understand how important it was to change her behavior. She also said she was removing her from the large group routine."

"And?" Heather whispered, wanting to hear how Kenna's mom had reacted.

"Oh my god! It wasn't pretty! Her mom totally defended Kenna and said that Kenna was the one being *ostracized* and that Gail was fostering a snotty attitude among the girls in her gym."

Kelley gasped. "Kenna? Left out? But she always goes off to work on her routines by herself. She never even stretches with the rest of the group!" Kelley couldn't believe anyone would criticize Gail. She was one of the nicest people Kelley had ever met.

"I *know*," Cadence said with great emphasis, *"Then* Kenna's mom said that my mom played favorites and that all she was interested in was *promoting her own daughter!"*

Heather and Kelley's mouths hung open. It was terrible to hear about Gail being accused of things that were so untrue.

"So how did she get anyone to believe this place is a fire hazard?"

"I'm not saying she did," Cadence smirked. "I'm just saying that Kenna's dad happens to be the Fire Chief."

"Whoa!" The girls gasped in unison.

"Could be a total coincidence though," Cadence muttered with a very sarcastic tone.

"So they're a whole family of bullies!" Kelley whispered.

"Pretty much," Cadence nodded.

"So," Gail said, speaking a bit more loudly now. "If I have permission from all you parents, I'd like to make today all about conditioning. We will run to the park, which is a good five-mile stretch. Then we'll work through our skills there. The girls will be ready for pick-up in two hours."

The girls let go a cheer and the parents all agreed to the plan.

"Okay!" Gail smiled. "Gymnasts! Everyone has to carry one piece of equipment."

Kelley grabbed a hoop while Cadence found a ball. Heather picked up a set of clubs and Natascha grabbed a rope.

"Is it okay for your nose if you jog?" Kelley asked Natascha.

"We'll see," she smiled. "If it hurts, I'll just walk. I'll catch up with you guys eventually!"

The girls took off after Gail as they began jogging through the village streets on the way to the park.

"We're like a Cirque du Soleil Circus troupe jogging into town," Kelley laughed.

"I wanna be in Cirque du Soleil!" Heather exclaimed and she leaped through the air.

"Me too!" Cadence joined in.

The girls ran, doing a variety of gymnastics as they went. It wasn't long before they were attracting a lot of attention. People applauded their tricks and a few kids even jogged along with them for a while.

They felt like a mini-parade. Kelley tossed the hoop up into the air as one little girl they passed shouted, "Do it again! Do it again!"

By the time they got to the park, they had an actual audience who stayed and watched the whole workout. Every skill, every movement earned applause and a few hoots.

Kelley felt happy and connected like she did when she was with her family. She was reminded again how good this group of girls was. They were going to have a great team, no matter who ended up getting selected.

The practice flew by with the help of the cheering crowd and as they warmed down, people started approaching Gail to ask for information.

"Looks like closing down the gym with lies and accusations might actually end up getting Gail some more business," said Kelley's mom as she walked up to the girls after the practice.

"Lemons out of lemonade!" Gail said as she joined them.

"How did you know it was lies, Mom?" Kelley asked.

"Well, you told me what went on last week with a certain someone... it wasn't hard to figure out."

"Onward and upward!" Gail said, obviously not wanting to dwell on the negative.

"Would you like a ride back to your car?" Kelley's mom asked Gail.

"Thanks! That would be great. In fact, anyone up for a late lunch?"

"Mexican!" Cadence called out.

"I guess so," her mom laughed and she headed toward the car.

It was more than an hour later when Kelley was relishing the last bites of her deep-fried ice cream that she suddenly sat straight up as if she'd just been poked.

"What?" Cadence said, alarmed.

"Jamie!" Kelley exclaimed. "She's waiting for me at the mall!"

Kelley ran to the car to get her phone. As she reached into her bag and searched for it, she held out a tiny hope that somehow Jamie might have forgotten too so they would both be able to forgive and forget. But as she lifted the phone out of the bag, that hope faded.

Six missed calls and four texts.

Kelley hurriedly shot off a text and then dialed Jamie's number. The call went directly to voicemail as Kelley's heart sank. Jamie had turned off her phone… not a good sign. After the beep, Kelley talked and talked, sputtering through apology after apology. She tried not to make excuses, because she knew no excuse in the world was good enough for standing up your best friend.

CHAPTER 11

The weekend seemed to last a year. As if it wasn't bad enough that her entire Rhythmics squad was waiting to hear about who was going to make the elite team, there was also the Fire Chief's inspection to worry about. And for Kelley, there was the fact that despite several texts and another five-minute apology message, Jamie still wasn't talking to her.

When she climbed into the Suburban after school, she heard the first good news she had heard in a while.

"I got a message from Gail," her mom said. "It appears the Fire Chief couldn't find any violations and the gym is open and waiting for you!"

"I knew they wouldn't find anything wrong," Kelley said.

"Still," her mom said, "it's good to have that cleared up!"

"Now we just have to wait on the Elite Team announcement and see if Jamie is ever going to speak to me again. Maybe if I spell out I'M SORRY in flower petals on her front lawn—"

"It's all going to work out, honey. You just have to be patient—with Jamie and with yourself! You might not make the elite team this time, but that doesn't mean you aren't doing really well."

Kelley tried to keep her mom's words in her head as she walked into the gym and saw all the girls gathered around a piece of paper posted on the wall. Clearly, the team had been announced. It was surprisingly quiet in the gym, but then that made perfect sense as Kelley thought about the fact that just as many girls didn't make the elite team as did.

It would be really unkind to celebrate in front of the girls who wouldn't get to compete.

As she walked toward the posted list, Cadence turned around and looked right at Kelley. Her expression was impossible to read. Either she was really excited because she made the team or nervous that Kelley was going to find out she didn't make the team or upset because she herself hadn't made the team or—

"We're both on!" Cadence whispered excitedly into Kelley's ear when she got close enough that she could squeeze her hand.

"Really?" Kelley responded in disbelief.

"See for yourself."

The group of girls seemed to part to make a path for Kelley to read the list. It was incredibly difficult to keep herself from squealing when she saw her name right below Cadence's on the list of five that also included Kenna, Heather, and Alexa.

"Congratulations!" Natascha was the first to talk to her.

Kelley looked back at the list. Natascha's name was not there. Kelley wished she could scratch out Kenna's name and replace it with Natascha's. But she also knew that Kenna would be an important part of the team. She may have been mean, but she was also a really good gymnast.

"It's okay," Natascha smiled through the face mask that was still protecting her broken nose. "I'm not really in the best shape to take on that much competition right now anyway. But I'm so happy for you guys!"

"You're the best," Kelley said to Natascha and then she hugged her carefully so as not to risk hurting her nose.

"Okay!" called out Gail, "you've all seen the list so now it's time to get down to business. Whether your name is on that list or not, we *all* have a lot of work to do!"

They went to work on the group routine and it felt great. Even though Kenna's probation left a hole at certain points of the choreography, all the girls were spot on. It was amazing to Kelley how much less tension she felt running through the routine without having to worry about making Kenna angry.

"It made it so much easier, didn't it?" said Cadence to Kelley as they were getting dressed after practice. "With Kenna out."

"I know!" Kelley agreed. "I didn't have to worry about her hissing at me for getting in her way so I could actually focus on just doing the best job I could in the routine!"

"It is amazing how one bully can wreck a whole group!" Heather added.

"I think I'm going to need your help," said a voice near the locker room door.

The girls turned to find Gail standing there. She had obviously overheard their conversation and a wave of nerves ran through Kelley as she wondered if they were about to get into trouble for gossiping.

"Hi, Mom," said Cadence nervously.

"I need the three of you to help me brainstorm a way to help Kenna be a better teammate. I can't kick her off the team, because she's technically advanced and her attendance is perfect. It's just her attitude that needs some serious adjustment."

"I don't know, Mom," Cadence said, shaking her head. "I think she *likes* being mean."

"Maybe not," Kelley said. "Maybe she just doesn't know *how* to be nice. I mean, if her mom really did report the gym for fire violations, then she obviously doesn't have a very good role model."

"That's very insightful, Kelley," said Gail. "So maybe we would all benefit from really getting clear on what we consider good team behavior."

"We could create a Team Code of Conduct!" declared Heather. "My school has one—it's like a private school, but it's totally not fancy— and every fall we have to sign an honor code promising to respect our fellow students and not cheat on exams or be late to class and stuff. At first I thought it was totally lame, but it actually kind of works. It holds everyone accountable for how they treat each other, you know? Like, you're more likely to respect the rules because you gave your word."

"Exactly!" agreed Gail.

"That sounds cool!" said Candace.

"And then we'll all sign a contract that says we'll follow it!" added Kelley.

"I knew you three could help me," Gail smiled. "Now get your stuff. It's time to go home."

Kelley beamed at her friends. They may not be able to change Kenna's attitude but maybe, just maybe, they could do something to help improve her behavior. And any small improvement in Kenna's attitude was sure to make the atmosphere in the gym more positive.

****

That night, Kelley sat on her bed making a list of the things she thought were most important when it came to being a good team member. "Don't throw clubs across the room. Don't put down gymnasts who aren't the same size as you. Don't say mean things." She was in the middle of writing, "Always do what you say you're going to do," when she heard a ding from her computer.

She clicked on Facebook and saw Jamie's name on an Instant Message. Kelley's heart beat a bit faster as she read the message, finding out just how mad her best friend was.

"Got all your messages. Sorry I didn't reply till now," the message said.

"I'm so sorry," Kelley typed.

"Yeah," Jamie replied. "I got that."

Kelley felt sick. Jamie sounded really mad and she couldn't blame her.

"Did it make sense when I tried to explain what happened?"

"Yup," Jamie typed. "I get it."

And then there was a long pause.

"But…?" Kelley typed, because she knew Jamie had more to say but was obviously holding back.

"But I'd be lying if I said my feelings weren't hurt. It's like you've just disappeared."

"I know," Kelley said, feeling ashamed of how little she'd done to stay in touch with the person who had been such a great friend to her. "I haven't been a very good friend in the last few weeks."

"What are you doing right now?" Jamie asked and Kelley felt a little ray of hope. Jamie was trying to change the subject. Maybe that meant she was willing to forgive her.

"Making a list of all the things that are important about being a good team member. Trying to help Kenna behave better!"

"Oh, yeah?" Jamie typed. "Like what?"

"The one I just wrote was, *Always do what you say you're going to do.*"

As Kelley hit SEND she realized how completely that applied to her and how she'd treated Jamie. There was a pause before Jamie replied.

"Ironic," Jamie wrote. Kelley held her breath until Jamie sent her a winking emoji. Then Kelley laughed out loud.

"Right?" Kelley typed and then she added a laughing emoji.

"Kenna sounds like a nightmare," Jamie typed. Then she sent Kelley an image of a fire-breathing dragon. "Nadia and Bethany combined were never that bad!"

"Ugh! The worst," Kelley responded and it felt so good to be talking to Jamie again.

"Mom?" Kelley shouted as she continued to chat with Jamie.

"What?" she called back from downstairs.

"Can I invite Jamie and her family to the lake for Thanksgiving weekend?"

There was a pause before her mom responded.

"Sure," she said. "That would be nice."

"Thank you so much, Mom!" Kelley called as she was already typing an invitation to Jamie.

"Hey!" she typed, "Will you and your family come to the lake with us for Thanksgiving? PLLEEEEEAASSEEE!" Kelley hoped Jamie knew how much she wanted her to say yes. A long weekend together, especially one as special as Thanksgiving, would definitely give them the time they needed to put their friendship back front and center where it belonged.

"Mom was just saying we didn't have plans," Jamie typed quickly. "I'll ask!"

"Yay!" responded Kelley. Then she said, "If we're lucky, Donovan (Cutest Neighbor Ever!) will be there!"

Jamie typed back a cheering emoji and then, "Gonna go ask my mom. BRB!"

As Kelley waited for Jamie to return, a message from Cadence popped up.

"We're going to be at the lake for Thanksgiving. Are you?" she wrote.

Kelley's high spirits fell again.

Two's company, three's a crowd, she thought. *Someone always feels left out.* But there was nothing she could do about it. *It worked the first weekend we all met,* she thought. *Maybe it'll be okay for Thanksgiving too.*

****

Kelley extended her arm and hoped that this time, the hoop would find her fingers. Then she heard it bounce on the mat behind her. She felt the burning in her eyes that always happened right before the tears. It had been a terrible and frustrating solo practice and she didn't want it to end before she got the new move Gail had taught her at least once.

It should be easy, Kelley thought. The hoop traveled along her leg as she did a walkover. Then she released the hoop off her foot, went into a toe-stand and caught it on her arm. *Except I haven't caught it, not once.* And by the end of her practice when she was feeling most frustrated, the rest of the team started showing up for group practice.

"You'll get it, Kelley," Gail finally said. "Let's move on to group."

Kelley couldn't respond, she just tried to smile and nodded. Cadence and Heather each took her by an arm.

"Do not feel bad!" Cadence insisted. "These hard days always happen right before you make a huge leap forward. It's just the way it works."

"You're just throwing it a little behind you," said Heather. "Once you start releasing it a beat sooner, you're going to rock it."

Kelley felt the frustration fade. "Thanks," she said, and she really meant it. She looked at both of them and suddenly felt incredibly lucky to be a part of the team, not just for the sport, but because these girls were turning into really good friends.

Suddenly, she felt Heather's arm pull roughly away from hers. The three girls all turned their heads just as Kenna pushed her way through the group, very much on purpose.

"First day back from probation and that's how you behave?" Heather snapped at her.

"Seriously?" Cadence called out. "Excuse you, Kenna!"

"Okay," called out Gail, "everyone gather round. I've had enough questionable behavior this month to last me all year. So, we are going to implement a code of conduct, which we will all help to create. Then we are each going to sign a contract that says we agree and we understand the consequences if we don't live by the code."

A round of excited whispers circled the group of the girls. It was clear that everyone thought this was a very good idea. It was also clear that everyone was trying really hard not to stare at Kenna.

"You are each to think about this at home tonight and bring me your ideas tomorrow. I want this done before we break for Thanksgiving in two weeks. Understood?"

The girls all nodded and a round of applause broke out that carried them into a great practice session. The code of conduct seemed to act as a motivator to really come together as a team and amazingly, they actually got most of the choreo down by the end of practice.

Kelley and Cadence headed to the locker room.

"I hate to admit it," Kelley said quietly, "but having Kenna back really helps the team."

Cadence nodded, smiled and shrugged her shoulders and Kelley understood perfectly. She might have had a few other things to say, but they were following the Code of Conduct now and trash talk was off the table!

Kelley felt her spirits lift. It was nice not to have to worry about the nastiness factor. She couldn't wait to tell Jamie about her day and that gave her spirits another boost. Things were back on track with her best friend and that was the best feeling in the world.

CHAPTER 12

"Paper. Pencil. Paper. Pencil," Cadence sounded as though she was selling peanuts at a baseball game as she went from girl to girl handing out a piece of paper and a pencil to each of them.

The girls were chatting up a storm as they discussed all the ideas they'd come up with for the Code of Conduct. Excitement was running high as they waited for Gail who was still in her office.

"She's unpacking the costumes," Cadence said breaking from her "paper, pencil" chant.

"The competition costumes?" Alexa jumped into the conversation.

"They're here already?" Natascha asked.

Cadence nodded and the buzz in the room grew even louder.

Kelley stole a glance at Natascha. She knew she'd been dreading the fitting and, in fact, she was the only girl not chattering excitedly. Kelley gave a smile and Natascha smiled back and rolled her eyes.

Gail's office door opened, and she emerged carrying a large box. She set the box down and hustled over to the girls.

"Okay, I want everyone to be heard equally no matter if you are shy or chatty or something in between. So, I've come up with a plan!"

Kelley couldn't help but smile. Gail was always so upbeat and positive; she couldn't help but feel better when Gail was around.

"So you each have a piece of paper that includes ten rules that I'm suggesting and three blank lines where you can add your own ideas."

"What if we have *more* than three suggestions?" Kenna blurted out.

"Like *don't interrupt!*" Cadence whispered to Kelley.

Kelley bit her lip to keep from smiling.

"Then I suggest you choose the three suggestions you think will be most helpful to the entire team," Gail said in a calm voice, but it was clear she didn't appreciate being interrupted. "If everyone would please go through my list of ten suggestions and check each of the ideas you agree with before adding your own, I will go through everyone's sheets and create a new list that includes the ten ideas that have the most votes. Majority rules!" she said with a smile. "Take a few minutes now to go through the list and when you're done, come see me for your costume fitting."

Gail left the girls to review the list and returned to sorting the costumes. Kelley sat down with Cadence, Heather, and Natascha and starting reading through the list.

Show up on time.

Conversation is to be held until the end of practice unless it is relevant to practice.

Negative comments about team members are prohibited anywhere in the gym.

Medical absence is the only acceptable reason for absence without advance notice.

Absence with advance notice will only be permitted twice per season and never within a month of competition.

Costume and class fees must be up to date for those who wish to compete.

No swearing

No bullying

No cell phones except in lobby.

No junk food in the gym.

Kelley could tell they all got to number ten at just about the same time, because all the girls started to groan.

"Well, everything but that one!" she heard someone say.

Cadence rolled her eyes and said, "that's my mom!"

Kelley laughed but she checked number ten along with all the rest because like it or not, she knew it was the right choice.

"Seems like a good code to me," Kelley said to Cadence.

"I'm good with it," Natascha agreed.

"Let's go get fitted!" Alexa jumped up, excited to try on her costume.

Natascha groaned.

Kelley grabbed Natascha's hand. "Come on! It won't be so bad!"

"Easy for you to say!"

The girls headed over to Gail, leaving behind several other teammates who were obviously spending more time adding their own ideas.

"Cadence," Gail said, holding out a costume. Cadence held up the leo and Kelley was reminded of how sheer they were. But she was happy to see that there actually was a lining, even though it was made to look as if there was none.

"Alexa... Natascha... Kelley..." Gail continued to hand out the costumes.

Natascha held up the costume. "There's no way a bra will work with this," Natascha said quietly as they headed to the locker room. "I know you skinny-stick girls can get away with that but I can't! It would not— ugh, I can't even think about it!"

"Watch who you're calling a stick girl," Cadence teased.

"Well, my mom doesn't let me wear anything without a bra and underwear, so we're in the same boat," Heather said as she looped her arm in Natascha's. "Besides, there is a lining. We might be able to sneak a bra in!"

Once in the locker room, they each found a private spot and starting pulling on the leos. Natascha hesitated. She moved close to Kelley and spoke quietly.

"Does it sound bitter if I think part of the reason I didn't make the elite team is because of the way I look in the costumes?"

Kelley looked at Natascha. She had been such a good sport about the elite team that Kelley realized she hadn't really looked at the situation from Natascha's point of view.

"No," she said quietly back to Natascha, "you don't sound bitter. I'm really sorry you're not on the team. You would be a great addition."

Priya was the first to get the costume on. She wrapped her arms around her middle, obviously feeling a little self-conscious.

"Maybe we just wear thongs," she said and everyone burst out laughing.

"Oh," chirped Heather, "my mother would *love* that!"

"I actually think they look great!" Alexa said as she looked around the locker room at the various girls as they each finished putting on the costume.

"You look really good in the costume!" Cadence said to Natascha.

"Sure!" she smiled. "If we're doing a commercial for cleavage!"

"Don't worry!" Cadence responded. "There's plenty of time for alterations."

They all piled out of the locker room to get a look at themselves in the big gym mirrors. Kelley stood with Cadence on one side of her and Natascha on the other.

"If you need alterations, come see me one at a time," Gail announced as she set up a measuring station in the corner of the gym.

There was no question the bodysuit was better on some bodies than on others. Kelley tried not to be too obvious as she allowed herself to look up and down the line of reflections in the mirror.

It was revealing, no doubt! That worked well on some of the girls but the cutout sections didn't hit the right spot on every girl's body. Those with longer torsos were having trouble making the cutaways not hit in such a way that they revealed too much chest. Kelley couldn't help but notice that as far as the fit was concerned, she and Cadence and Heather were the luckiest.

"Mine is way too big," whined Kenna. "It's baggy on the bottom and the top."

All focus went to Kenna who seemed to be secretly happy that she could complain about how big the leo was on her, especially since she was standing next to Natascha.

"I wish I couldn't see her six-pack through the fabric!" Cadence whispered.

Kelley nodded, wishing too that she didn't feel a twinge of jealousy at Kenna's incredibly toned physique.

Gail was busy marking up the leos that needed alteration. Taking Natascha's measurements took some time since she was going to need an entirely new bodice to allow for coverage of her chest.

"If Natascha would just get a boob job, we could have been halfway through practice by now," Kenna said in a voice loud enough for the girls to hear but not loud enough for Gail to hear.

Kelley realized there was something that should be added to the code of conduct. She walked over to where the pile of papers were and found hers. On the first of the three blank lines she wrote, "If a team member hears or sees another team member breaking the code, that team member is obligated to report the behavior."

Kelley slipped her paper back into the pile. She turned and stared at Kenna. The feeling of empowerment that came over her in that moment carried her all the way through practice.

This is what I've been missing, she thought at the end of a tough practice, *the way teammates look out for each other—because we are not* ten *people, we are* one *team!*

CHAPTER 13

"I am *so* ready for Thanksgiving break!" Natascha declared as she pulled her hair back on their way out of the locker room.

"One more week," Kelley said and it was clear she would be ready for the break too. "I could hardly get out of bed this morning," she added.

The girls had been practicing hard and Kelley could tell just by looking around that they were all tired. Her gaze fell on Kenna who was already out on the floor practicing with the clubs. *She always gets in practice before the group session,* thought Kelley. *No wonder she's so amazing!*

Kelley couldn't help but stare at the girl as she nailed one move after another. She *never* dropped a club and every bit of her body was in perfect form from pointed toes to outstretched arms.

"Annoying, isn't it?" whispered Cadence as she slipped in next to Kelley to watch Kenna practice.

"I know it's wrong, but I really wish she wouldn't be soooo good. I hate when mean people are good at things. It's not fair," Kelley said as quietly as she possibly could.

She felt Cadence stifle a giggle.

"Karma can take a long time to catch up with bullies," Cadence said equally quietly.

"Do you think karma could keep her from winning this season?"

The two girls watched as Kenna threw both clubs up in the air at the same time but somehow got them to fall back into her grasp at two different times—the first after one pirouette, the second after a second pirouette.

Kelley's question hung in the air. Could she possibly *not* win this season?

"No," Cadence said after witnessing the spectacular catch. "I think karma is going to have to wait for another opportunity!"

"I have a hoop waiting for me!" Kelley declared, realizing she shouldn't be standing around complaining about how good her nemesis was. She should be working on getting better herself.

Kelley had been following Kenna's lead and grabbing every last minute of practice she could. She'd been improving steadily and finally mastered the hoop catch that had so frustrated her last week. That had been a real turning point. Her confidence had grown enormously and now the rest of her routine was fully choreographed. She couldn't wait to be able to really practice it from beginning to end. Her ball, clubs, and ribbon routines were simpler, but they were taking a lot of focused time too. She didn't feel so naturally comfortable with those as she did with the hoop, so even simple choreo took her longer to master.

"We'll start with group in ten minutes," Gail announced from the threshold of her office. "Use this time wisely, girls!"

The girls scattered, each struggling to find enough space for herself to really run through elements. Kelley tried to claim a corner of the mat on which Kenna was working, but the bully intentionally threw a club in the air so that she had to leap and land right in front of Kelley as the club fell back down into her hand inches from Kelley's head.

"Oh, gee," smiled Kenna. "Sorry about that. Guess you'd better find somewhere else to practice."

A flitter of activity over by Gail's office grabbed Kelley's attention before she could say anything she might regret in reply to Kenna. Girls were gathering around Gail as she taped something to the wall.

"Oh, look," she said, turning to Kenna and staring her right in the eye. "It looks as though Gail is posting the code of conduct."

Kenna glared at her.

"Might be a good idea for you to go read through it," Kelley said. "You wouldn't want to get kicked off the team for bad behavior." Kelley was pleased with herself that she had found such a positive way to let Kenna know that she'd just behaved very badly. Kelley turned and walked away from her. She wanted to read the list herself and find out which rules made the final cut. She wondered if her last-minute addition would be on the list.

"No Junk Food was voted down!" Heather sang out as Kelley reached the group of girls reading through the list. "Good thing since I would have broken that rule anyway!"

The girls nodded in agreement.

"Yeah, but," Alexa said grabbing her attention, "she added No Gum."

"I can live without gum," Heather replied. "I just can't live without chips!"

Kelley scanned the list. There were eleven rules in all. Each of the original ten suggestions were still on the list except for the junk food rule. As she looked the bottom, she saw the No Gum rule. Then she saw the very last rule, it was the one she had suggested.

If a team member hears or sees another team member breaking the code then that team member is obligated to report the behavior.

She looked back at Kenna who was still on the mat practicing. *Just wait,* Kelley thought, *if karma won't get you, number eleven will!*

CHAPTER 14

"Thanksgiving is my favorite holiday," said Jamie as she carefully placed a tiny dried purple flower into the very center of a little bouquet held within a miniature pumpkin.

The air was thick with the amazing smells that only seem to exist at the end of November—roasting turkey, sweet warm pumpkin, baking apples, and endless butter and cream! There was laughter and chatter filling the house as Kelley's and Jamie's families all prepared for the big meal. Jamie's mom and grandma were in the kitchen with Kelley's parents telling stories as they put the finishing touches on the dinner they'd all prepared. Kelley was grateful that Jamie's grandma was healthier than the year before and able to join them for another holiday. She knew Jamie was too.

"Mine too... along with Christmas, Halloween, Easter, Fourth of July, Valentine's Day, Groundhog Day and of course, Flag Day," Kelley replied. "Oh, and Memorial Day!"

"And of course, of *course*, MOTHER's Day!" her mom added as she swept into the room with two water pitchers.

"Of *course!*" laughed Kelley. "I meant to say that one first!"

"I know you did, dear," her mom winked as she headed back to the kitchen to continue preparations for the feast.

"My mom loves Thanksgiving too," Kelley said nodding to her as she went. "She's always in the best mood on this day."

Jamie picked up another miniature pumpkin to begin working on for the last of the six centerpieces the girls were making. She selected the blooms she wanted to put in the pumpkin from the pile of flowers they'd gotten yesterday from the market in town. But before she started arranging them, she stopped and looked at Kelley who couldn't help but notice that she had an odd look in her eye.

"What?" Kelley smiled.

"I'm just really glad you invited my mom, *Abuelita,* and me. I know it's only been a little over a year since we moved to Seattle, but it just feels like home being here with you and your family."

Kelley was surprised at the sudden lump in her throat. Jamie was really one of the best friends she'd ever had. She was just as happy that they were here, especially when she thought back on the rocky transition they'd survived with Kelley's move away from Kip's.

"Wouldn't have it any other way!" Kelley said, fighting down the lump in her throat. "Besides, without you, I'd eat all the sweet potatoes and then I'd never fit into my leo for competition."

Jamie elbowed her friend.

"Plus, you might even have a chance to meet the incredibly cute Donovan!" Kelley said.

"And see Cadence again," Jamie added. "I'm really glad she and her family are going to have dessert with us today. I liked her a lot when we met this summer! Besides, I need to know more about this girl who is spending so much time with my best friend."

"She's excited too!" Kelley nodded and then she felt a well of emotion swell up again. Jamie was so amazing, the way she just took things in stride. "You really are the best, you know that?"

Both girls laughed as they recognized they were both getting more emotional than they meant to.

"Okay!" declared Jamie, "We have centerpieces to make!"

"Where do we want the pilgrims?" Kelley's dad shouted as he and her brother crashed through the front door carrying life-size pilgrims made almost like scarecrows.

"Um, Dad?" Kelley said.

"What?" he answered, proud of the enormous figures they had made.

"I think Mom meant little figures to put around the turkey on the sideboard."

Kelley turned to look at her mother's face as she opened the swinging door that separated the kitchen from the dining room. Jamie's mom and grandmother were looking on from behind her. The expression on her mother's face was more than Kelley and Jamie could bear. They both fell into a round of hysterical laughter that soon spread to everyone in the room.

Jamie's right, Kelley thought as she started to regain her composure. *Thanksgiving really is the best holiday of the year!*

****

For the first time that day, everyone seemed to fall silent, except for the contented groans of Kelley's and Cadence's dads. Thanksgiving dinner was finished and every last morsel had been complete delicious. Everyone at the table—three families' worth—was feeling entirely stuffed.

"Why don't we eat pumpkin pie all year 'round?" Cadence asked as she stared at what was left in the tin, clearly considering another piece.

"I'm never going to be able to do an aerial anything tomorrow at practice," Jamie moaned, holding her belly.

"Well at least you don't have to try to fit inside a hoola hoop!" Kelley laughed. "Why did you let me have a second piece of pie?"

"She was too busy eating a second piece herself to stop you!" her mom chimed in.

"Why don't you kids roll yourselves outside while we clean up? It's almost 65 degrees out there for some strange reason. Might as well enjoy it!"

The four kids looked at each other as if the idea of standing up was more than they could bear. The girls rallied and dragged themselves up. Kelley's brother rolled onto the floor and much to everyone's amusement, crawled toward the door.

The weather really was amazing. It felt like an early September day even though December was right around the corner. The girls made their way slowly down to the water's edge as they talked about what lay ahead for them.

"So your competition team starts next week too?" Cadence asked Jamie.

"Yup," she nodded. "That's why we have to head back tonight. I have practice tomorrow and Saturday."

"So do we," Cadence replied.

"I'm really nervous about tomorrow," Kelley added. "We have to perform our solos for the rest of the team."

"Oh, you're in great shape!" Cadence said and knocked Kelley on the arm.

"She's always been tough on herself," Jamie told Cadence as she knocked Kelley on the other arm. "Remember that time you were convinced you'd never be able to land your dismount off the uneven bars and that you stuck a perfect landing? After having done like three of the hardest moves possible on bars?"

Kelley felt so good having two such good friends, one on either side of her. But before she could respond, she spied Donovan a little farther down along the beach. With no warning, she felt her heart beating faster and a warmth rise up in her cheeks.

"Ooooh!" squealed Cadence. "Look who's skipping stones!"

Just then, Donovan looked up and noticed them. He seemed to almost jump at the sight of them. He waved, grabbed the soccer ball that was sitting at his feet and started walking toward them.

Kelley felt her blush intensify as she waved back. But then she heard Jamie's voice behind her.

"Hey!" Jamie called as she quickened her pace and passed Kelley on her way to meet up with Donovan.

"Wait," said Kelley, confused, "what?"

"He goes to my school," Jamie said, turning to look at Kelley and Cadence.

"Really?" Kelley asked.

Jamie stopped, "*That's* the Donovan you've been talking about?"

Kelley felt her stomach flip as she recalled her endless chatter about Donovan on the drive up to the house yesterday. If she'd known he was Jamie's classmate, she might have kept her mouth shut. Why did she suddenly feel even more embarrassed?

"Shut up," Kelley said as Donovan neared. "Just be cool!"

"What are you all doing together?" Donovan smiled. "My worlds are colliding!"

"Kelley's been my best friend ever since we moved here!" Jamie declared.

Kelley tensed up for a moment, wondering if Cadence minded the "best friend" reference, but when she stole a glance at her, it was clear she wasn't bothered at all.

"We all do gymnastics," Cadence told Donovan.

"Anybody *do* soccer?" he asked as he dropped the ball and bounced it up onto his knee.

"I do!" Kelley replied as she stole the ball from Donovan and bounced it up from her knee to her head, down to her chest, and then let it roll down to her feet before popping it back up to him with her toe.

"Wow! Impressive!" he said with an extra nice smile at Kelley.

"Don't hog the ball!" Jamie called out as she ran a few yards away and Donovan kicked the ball in her direction.

"I'm not hogging the ball!" he laughed. "I'm not the one who thinks she's the only one who knows how to make a goal."

"I never said that!" Jamie argued.

"I'm not talking about you," he said as Cadence kicked the ball back to Jamie.

"Oooh…" Jamie said, rolling her eyes. "You mean our favorite soccer player from school?"

"What are you talking about?" Kelley asked as the four friends formed a circle and began passing the ball to one another.

"Just a girl from school who basically informs just about everyone that they should quit if they can't play as well as her."

"Hmmm," Cadence said. "That sounds remarkably familiar."

"We have a girl at the gym who loves to suggest that people should drop off the team too."

"Kenna," Cadence said at exactly the same moment that Donovan and Jamie offered up the name of the bully at their school… "Kenna!"

"Yours is Kenna too?" Kelley asked in disbelief.

"Really skinny girl with a big fat attitude?" Donovan asked Kelley.

"Yes! That's the one!" Candace squealed.

"Whoa! That is a scary coincidence," said Jamie, amazed.

"I can't believe we are all being tormented by the same Kenna!" Kelley laughed as the soccer ball flew toward her and she jumped up to head it back to Donovan.

"Nice shot!" Donovan cheered as he trapped the ball with his right foot only to immediately pass it to Jamie with his left. He seemed impressed with Kelley's skills for a second time.

Kelley was sure she was imagining it, but she thought he kept his eyes on her a beat longer than normal. Kelley tried not to study him too carefully but she couldn't help wondering if he being a little friendlier to her than he was to everyone else.

"Nice save!" he called out as Jamie lunged for the ball to keep it from heading toward the water.

Kelley stared at him as long as she could without being obvious. There was something about his shoulders and the athletic way he moved with the ball that captured her attention. *No*, she thought, *he's just a nice guy and he's treating everyone the same.* She looked away as soon as she sensed he was looking back toward her. She felt his eyes on her as she ran to get the ball.

Or... maybe not, she thought. Boys! *Who knows?*

"Hey, pass me the ball!" Jamie called. "I want to try to hit it with my head."

"It's called a header," Kelley said as she tossed the ball gently to Jamie. "Hit the ball with the top of your forehead. Anywhere else and you could get hurt."

Jamie jumped up to header the ball and totally missed. "Guess I'll stick with gymnastics.

"Nah," said Cadence. "Here, I'll practice with you."

Kelley suddenly flushed as her friends moved away leaving her alone with Donovan. It seemed almost as if they had done it on purpose.

Now that it was just the two of them, Kelley suddenly felt awkward, like she had to think really hard to come up with something to say.

"So you, play a team?" she finally asked as the two of them began walking along the lakeshore.

"Um, yeah," Donovan said, looking down at his feet.

He seemed nervous, but Kelley couldn't tell if it was because he liked being alone with her or wished the other girls would come back.

"You?" he asked.

"I used to," Kelley said. "Now I just play pick-up and in a few tournaments over the weekend. I had to let something go when I decided to focus on gymnastics. But I really—"

"You must miss it," Donovan said as Kelley finished her sentence.

"Miss it," they both said at the same time. "Jinx!" Kelley and Donovan giggled.

"Kelley, I—" Donovan began.

"Girls, it's time to come in!" Kelley's mom's voice interrupted them. "Kelley, where are you?"

Kelley thought she could detect a note of concern in her mom's voice. "I'd better go."

"Yeah," said Donovan. "It was good to see you."

"You too"

Kelley ran to catch up with her friends.

"So who was the boy who was walking alone with my daughter by the lake?" Kelley's mom asked as the girls scooted past her and into the house.

"Mooooom!"

"That's Donovan," said Candace. "His grandmother lives next door."

"Do you have a crush on this boy?"

Kelley felt the heat rise to her cheeks.

"I, um—" Suddenly, Kelley felt as tongue-tied as she had talking to Donovan.

"He goes to my school," said Jamie. "He's super-cool and his mom is really nice." Kelley silently thanked her friend for stepping in just when she needed help—as usual. She knew her mom was half-joking, but she was not ready to have this conversation.

Kelley's mom raised her eyebrows but didn't say anything.

"So who's ready for second dessert?" Candace asked.

"Me!" Jamie called, looping one arm through Kelley's. "All that soccer playing left me famished! Right Kel?"

And with that, all three girls skipped off into the kitchen.

CHAPTER 15

"Take a deep breath," Kelley's mom said as they pulled into the gym parking lot. "You're gonna be great. You always are."

"I can't believe how nervous I am!" Kelley said as she took a minute before getting out of the car.

Saturday morning practice had arrived; each girl would be performing her solo in front of everyone else for the first time. Kelley had practiced almost constantly since getting back from Thanksgiving at the lake. She wanted Gail to know that she had made the right choice by putting her on the elite team. But Kelley realized she needed to prove that to herself too. She'd come a long way in a short time with Rhythmic, but she'd never done any of it under the pressure of performance. This morning would be her first taste of that.

"Double time, girls!" Gail was calling out as Kelley walked through the door. "We have a lot to do today. Solo performances, Code of Conduct review, and group practice. So get changed extra quick!"

The nerves and excitement were showing on everyone. It was particularly quiet as everyone changed into their leos. Natascha seemed easily frustrated when she couldn't get her hair just right in her bun. Heather appeared to be misplacing everything. And Kenna didn't even bother to sneer at anyone. She kept her head down as she headed out to the floor.

"Is everyone as nervous as I am?" Kelley said out loud, and she could feel all the girls take a collective deep breath.

"It looks like it!" Cadence laughed.

They all headed out to take their place along the edge of the mat where they would watch, one after another, each of the girls perform. As Kelley studied the focused faces that circled the mat, she realized it wasn't just their own performances they were all nervous about executing for the first time. It was also the fact that they'd be seeing their competition for the first time too. They were a team but they were also individual performers and everyone wanted to be the best!

"Okay! I want each of you to take a minute to tell yourself what a great job you've done to get to this point. I know you are all nervous and that's okay. Nerves can be a good motivation in performance. But this is just the beginning, so try to relax a little and enjoy your first chance to nail your routine!"

The girls laughed at the idea that they might relax but they all smiled too. Perhaps they were relaxing just a touch!

Candace grabbed Kelley's hand and gave it a squeeze. Her smile seemed to say, "I know you are going to be amazingly awesome!"

Kelley squeezed back. She knew Candace was going to be fabulous. She always was.

"Okay, let's get going. I have everyone's name written on a slip of paper in this envelope. I'm going to call you up as I pick your name so there's absolutely no significance to the order."

The whole team seemed to tense up again as Gail's hand plunged into the envelope. She pulled out a slip of paper and read the name written on it.

"Heather!"

All eyes went to Heather as she accepted her fate as "first up." She picked up her ribbon and positioned herself in the center of the mat. She waited for Gail to begin her music as the room was so quiet Kelley could hear her heart beating.

From the first note of music, Heather was like a continuous swirling extension of the ribbon. She began with a series of pirouettes while the ribbon encircled her entire body and from there she tossed the ribbon so easily into the air, Kelley was amazed when it fell in a perfect spiral back into her hand as she completed an aerial front walkover into a forward roll. Her flexibility and grace were astonishing. Kelley remembered back to the demo she had seen before make the decision to take up Rhythmic. Heather's performance had been a big part of what had convinced her that this would be a wonderful sport. Watching her again today, it was clear to Kelley why she had been so impressed. Heather was a wonderful performer. The enthusiastic applause that erupted as she hit her final pose made it clear that Kelley was not the only one who found Heather inspiring.

Kelley felt a tinge of jealousy as Heather stepped off the mat—not because of how good she was at rhythmic, but because she had her solo debut performance out of the way. Kelley just wanted to get hers over with so she could exhale!

"Cadence!" Gail called out.

"Ugh!" Cadence responded without a moment's hesitation and everyone laughed.

"You're going to be great!" Kelley said as Cadence walked to the mat.

She hit her opening position with her arm held straight up in the air and the ball perched perfectly on the palm of her hand. There was a quiet moment and then the heavy beat of her music filled the air. Cadence exploded off the mat with an amazing jeté as the ball sailed up into the air only to be caught in the small of her back as she rolled onto the floor. Kelley smiled as she watched her friend cover the mat with her fast, syncopated movements. She was so different from Heather. It was as if Heather was a ballet dancer and Cadence was more Hip Hop. Kelley's style was closer to Heather's but she loved watching the fun Cadence seemed to have with her routine.

The applause rang out as Cadence hit her final post but Kelley stopped hearing anything once Gail read the next name pulled out of the bag.

"Kelley!"

It was as if the noise was pulled from the air. All Kelley could hear was the sounds inside her body as she walked to the center of the mat. She heard the beat of her heart, the rush of her blood, the pad of her feet on the mat. She remembered what it had felt like to step out onto the mat for her floor routine during Nationals. The confidence of knowing that she had worked her hardest in training and whatever happened on that mat during the performance was only one moment in a long string of performances and practices. She pictured her gymnastics career like a ribbon making waves in the air, constantly changing but always awe inspiring. She imagined what Nadia would do in a moment like this and raised her chin a little higher. She heard Jamie's voice in her head saying, "You've SO got this." And suddenly Kelley felt as though she *did* have this. She wasn't nervous. She was confident. Hoop was her thing.

Kelley positioned her hoop on the ground so that it rested exactly right on her foot. She struck her opening pose and waited for the sound of her music. In that instant, her eyes fell on Kenna's face staring up at her from the edge of the mat. *Ignore it,* she told herself. She took her starting position on the ground. She felt like a snake with her legs pressed together against the mat, her upper body lifted and the hoop held above her head in both outstretched arms. She closed her eyes and then she heard her music. An Argentine tango.

At least it's not country western music, she thought.

Kelley twirled the hoop with her right hand then rocked her body forward raising her legs so she could pull the hoop behind her. As she worked through the very first movements, the ones that had kept her so frustrated a week or two ago, she felt every muscle as it contracted and released. She twirled the hoop around her next as she rose up to her feet, like a figure skater doing a camel spin. Then the hoop sailed into the air. She extended her reach and felt it land perfectly. From there, the tension just melted away and she fell so fully into her choreography that she didn't even have to think about it. She loved this routine. She loved Gail's choreography and how well it fit her body. Kelley stepped in and through her hoop and twirled it with her left ankle. She kicked it up into the air as she would a soccer ball and caught it around her wrist, spinning it the whole time. Her extension was perfect, her limbs long and limber just as they'd always been on beam. She tumbled across the mat, the hoop a perfect extension of her arm and moved through each element without a hitch. When she tossed the hoop up into the air, twirled, and struck her final pose as the hoop landed gracefully in her outstretched hand, Kelley was surprised to find herself standing there on the other side of the performance, a tiny bit out of breath, and whole lot proud of herself.

Did I do everything? she wondered. The whole performance was a blur. She knew she hadn't dropped the hoop, but that was about all she was certain of.

But then she heard her teammates' applause and Gail exclaiming, "Wonderful!"

"Amazing!" Cadence and Heather called out.

"Excellent job, Kelley!" Gail continued. "You sailed right through those challenging spots and you are really handling the hoop well!"

Kelley couldn't believe what she was hearing. Had it really gone that well? She knew she still had work to do. The hoop needed to feel like an absolute extension of her arm and not a piece of equipment. But she had sort of felt that way toward the end, and she was getting closer to maintaining that feeling every day!

Gail's words were ringing in her ears as she backed away from the center of the mat. It felt so good to not only be through that first performance but to have felt better doing it than she ever had—

"OWWW!" a howl of pain rang out as she stumbled over something at the edge of the mat.

"My foot! My foot!"

The shouts pulled Kelley from her post-performance fog. She looked down to realize in horror what she had stumbled over. Her foot had landed directly on top of Kenna's foot and then she had stepped down fully with all her weight! Kenna was curled in a ball holding her foot and ankle. Her face was bright red as she cried out in pain.

"Oh, no!" Kelley exclaimed. "I'm sorry! I'm so sorry!"

"Ooohh!" wailed Kenna as the team all gathered around her.

"Let me see!" Gail called out and the girls made way for their coach.

"You broke my ankle!" Kenna cried as she continued to writhe in pain.

"It was an accident!" Kelley whimpered. "What can I do?"

The horror of what she'd done grew clearer and clearer as Kelley stood helplessly watching Gail try to calm Kenna down. She could already see the ankle was swelling and turning a light purple.

"I don't think it's broken," Gail said calmly. "But we do need to get it looked at."

Priya ran to get and ice pack, which Gail wrapped expertly around Kenna's foot.

Kelley silently scolded herself for not having gone for the ice pack herself. She felt paralyzed as she watched the scene unfold. All she had ever wanted was to steer clear of Kenna entirely. Now she had done the worst thing possible.

What if Kenna can't perform? Kelley thought. *I could have just ruined things for the entire team!*

How had such a wonderful moment turned so quickly into such a terrible one?

"Cadence, come hold the ice pack in place," Gail said. "I have to call Kenna's mom."

"I'm really sorry," Kelley repeated as Gail hurried by her. She felt Natascha place an arm around her shoulder as her eyes filled with tears. Kelley wished she could just disappear.

****

It felt like a hundred years before her mom pulled up to the front door of the gym. Kelley crawled into the front seat and slunk down in her seat as her mom handed her a Vitamin Water—the flavor was Revive. She had sent her mom a text telling her what had happened so she didn't have to say a thing as they drove out of the parking lot. That was a good thing since Kelley knew she would burst out crying if she tried to talk. Kelley took a sip of her Vitamin Water and leaned her forehead against the cool glass of the window. Kenna's mom had shown up to get Kenna ranting about how dangerous the gym was and how everyone should be ashamed of themselves. Kelley couldn't even make eye contact let alone apologize for injuring her daughter.

Kelley cringed at the memory. She pulled out her phone hoping to find something that might distract her just long enough to get her home where she could go up to her room and be alone.

Kelley smiled slightly to see a text from Jamie. Somehow her friend always knew when she needed to hear from her most. "Hey! Donovan wants your number!!! Do I have permission to give it to him?"

Kelley stared out the window as they drove home. If the memory of her first successful solo performance wasn't enough to make her feel good today, Donovan's attention wasn't going to do it either. Kelley closed her eyes again, trying to change what had happened with the power of visualization. If only she hadn't been so distracted. If only she'd been looking where she was going. If only—

Kelley's phone buzzed in her lap.

Another text from Jamie.

"Just thinking about how awesome you are, Bestie! Hope you killed it on hoop!"

And even though she didn't want to, Kelley allowed herself to smile just a little.

CHAPTER 16

Kelley had to think about every step to get herself back through the doors of the gym on Monday. She was grateful to have had yesterday to hide away in her room—happy to take whatever distance she could from the terrible moment on Saturday when she'd stepped on Kenna's foot. She'd accidentally crashed into girls on the soccer field before, but that was the risk of playing soccer. Sometimes you got knocked down. Sometimes you twisted an ankle or accidentally headed the back of someone's head instead of the ball. It felt awful, but it was part of the game. Getting stepped on was not a part of gymnastics, Rhythmic or Artistic. With all the other risks a squad took, they should be able to trust their teammates to be more careful.

Secretly, Kelley hoped everyone had magically forgotten what she'd done and that they'd all just start practice as usual. But her hopes plummeted when she walked in and saw Kenna and her mother in Gail's office. Kenna's ankle looked terrible all wrapped up. *Could it possibly still be that swollen?* she wondered. *Or is the bandaging making it look so thick?*

Kelley ran into the locker room, her head spinning with ideas of sneaking out the back door. She couldn't face Kenna or her mother! She turned to see Cadence, Priya, and Heather staring at her.

"I take it you saw Kenna and her mom?" Cadence asked.

"Her ankle looks as though it's even more swollen than it was on Saturday!" Kelley answered.

"I'm sure it's just wrapped really well," Priya said. "We all know it was an accident, Kelley."

"Don't be so hard on yourself," Heather said as she put an arm around Kelley. "It could have happened to any of us."

"Get changed," Cadence told her. "We'll wait for you."

Kelley hurried to her locker and made fast business out of getting ready for practice before heading back out to join her friends.

"Thank you," she said, taking a moment to look at each of them. "I do feel *really* awful about this and it helps to know you guys believe it was a total accident."

The four girls linked arms as they made their way out of the locker room. But as soon as the door closed behind them, they heard angry shouts coming from Gail's office.

"Yikes!" Priya whispered.

"You created this Code of Conduct. Why don't you use it? Or was it just to make Kenna feel uncomfortable?" Kenna's mother was continuing to speak in a very angry tone. The girls froze in their tracks.

"You don't allow bullying?" Kenna's mom barked. "Then kick that girl *off the team*! She stepped on my daughter. That is obvious bullying!"

Before Kelley could stop them, her friends dropped their hold on her arms to step up and defend her against the bullying accusations.

"Kelley is *not* a bully!" Cadence said firmly. "It was a total accident!"

"Kenna was sitting right next to me," Priya added. "There was no way that was on purpose!"

"Okay, girls!" Gail jumped in as Kenna's mom's face grew ever more red with fury. "Go stretch out and I'll be with you in just a moment." As Gail stepped over to the girls and away from Kenna and her mother, she briefly put her arm around her daughter's shoulder. She whispered, "It's not going to happen, don't worry!"

Heather took a breath, about to say something more, but Cadence took her by the arm. "Come on!" she said. "Leave it to my mom."

Gail turned back to Kenna's mother, "I am so sorry that Kenna got injured. We all are. She's a very important part of our team and it's the last thing anybody would want! Why don't you and I talk about this in my office?"

Gail calmly led them into her office, leaving Kenna sitting on a chair just outside. The girls turned back toward Kenna and cautiously walked over to her as if they were approaching a wild animal.

"Hi, Kenna," Cadence said carefully. "Are you in a lot of pain?

"What did the doctor say?" Heather asked.

Kelley tried to speak but found the lump had returned to her throat. She did not want to cry in front of everyone.

"It's sprained," Kenna said just as her mother's voice spiked again in rage. Kelley thought she saw Kenna almost cringe at the sound of her mother's anger but then she spoke loudly herself, almost as if she was trying to drown out the sound of her mom. "But of course, everyone knows sprains are more painful than breaks." Kenna leaned over and pulled a pair of crutches out from under her chair.

Kelley gasped. Somehow the crutches made it all even worse. She looked at her teammates' faces and could see they all shared her fear. What if Kenna really couldn't compete? What would happen to their group routine? And what if Kelley really did get kicked off the team? It would be impossible for them to compete at all!

Just then, the door of Gail's office flew open and Kenna's mother stormed out.

"I guess your code of conduct is only for the girls you don't like!" her mother growled. Then she grabbed Kenna by the arm and nearly made her tumble over her crutches. "Kenna! We're leaving!" she snapped. She pulled her daughter toward the front door in a way that made it hard to tell if she was pushing or dragging her. But either way, it was clear she was incredibly angry.

As the door shut behind them, Kelley felt the color drain from her face. She felt a little dizzy but couldn't explain why. She slowly sat down in the chair where Kenna had been.

"She will calm down," Gail said, comforting the shell-shocked girls. "I promise you, it will all work out." She turned to look at Kelley who couldn't hold back the tears any longer. They fell silently down her cheeks. "The code does not apply here, Kelley. We all know that Kenna was not being bullied. It was an accident."

Kelley nodded. She was grateful for Gail's soothing tone, but it didn't help her shake the horrible feeling that someone thought she was a bully. She had never in her life been accused of hurting someone on purpose and it felt like the worst thing in the world!

CHAPTER 17

"So... she was just sitting there waiting when you and your mom arrived?" Heather spoke to Cadence in a hushed voice as the girls changed into their practice leos the next day.

"Weird, right?" Cadence's eyes were wide as she nodded. "Her mom wasn't waiting with her and the crutches were gone and she just sort of smiled at us when we walked up to the door."

"Smiled?" Priya confirmed.

"Yes," Cadence whispered, amazed. "And it was a real smile too. Like she meant it!"

"So was she limping?" Kelley asked. She wanted to hear that Kenna was perfectly fine, that it had all been an act. It would mean Kenna was horrible and mean but it would also mean that Kelley didn't have to think about the fact that she had really hurt someone.

"She was," Cadence said quietly. "No crutches, but she's definitely still feeling a little uncomfortable."

Kelley dropped her gaze and nodded.

"But she's back!" Heather said, putting a hand on Kelley's back. "That's the really important part. Her mom's not making her drop off the team and since she's not here screaming about the Code of Conduct maybe she's chilled out about that too!"

"Yeah," said Cadence as she threw all her stuff in her locker and closed it, ready to get to the gym. "I don't know what's up with her mom. It was a little odd that she just left Kenna there."

"It's all a little odd!" Priya declared as the group of girls headed for the mats.

The conversation went quiet as the entered the gym. Kenna was sitting on the edge of the mat. She held two clubs and was marking her arm choreo around her club tosses. When she sensed she was not alone, she turned and looked at the girls. Kelley braced herself for whatever mean thing Kenna was about to say. She figured she'd have to endure a lot of meanness before she and Kenna were on even ground again. But Kenna just smiled at everyone and turned back around, minding her own business.

The girls exchanged looks, each more puzzled than the last.

"Who are you and what have you done with Kenna?" Cadence whispered to Kelley. Normally, Kelley would have had to fight back the giggles but not today. Today, she was (once again) too busy fighting back tears.

Gail opened the storage closet and start pulling out props. Before Kelley even registered what was happening, Kenna got quickly to her feet.

"I can help you," she said to Gail and she hurried over to the closet, clearly favoring her ankle but not making a scene about it.

Gail's expression was one of pure surprise. The girls couldn't stop staring. It really was as if someone completely different was wearing a Kenna costume. Whoever this was, it wasn't the Kenna they all knew!

"Anyone else going to help?" Gail called out, more to get everyone to stop staring at Kenna than anything else.

The girls jumped, pulled out of their stunned silence.

"Of course!'

"Sure!"

"Right here!"

They all clamored to help set up for practice.

"So it looks like you're feeling a little better," Cadence was the first to break the ice and speak directly to Kenna.

Kenna nodded. "I just iced it, took a painkiller and told my mom I wanted to come back."

The girls nodded enthusiastically. None of them wanted to talk about her mom. Nobody wanted to land anywhere close to Kenna's mom's bad side!

"Well, it's nice to have you back!" Heather exclaimed.

Kenna looked at her, clearly grateful for her kind words. "Thanks," she said and then nothing else. No nasty put down. No sarcastic response.

Kelley desperately wanted to talk to her. Apologize again. Make sure she really did believe it was an accident. But every time she worked up enough courage to open her mouth someone else would speak. She was just about to try again when--

"Okay!" Gail said as she closed the closet and turned to the girls. "We have a lot of work today. Our first competition is only three days away! Kenna, we are delighted to have you back. I will remind you to take it very easy today. It's more important for you to take another day or two to heal than it is to practice your skills over and over. You're in great shape. You just have to trust that!"

Kenna smiled so sincerely that everyone found themselves just staring at her again. Throughout the practice, Kenna never had a bad thing to say about anything or anyone. She was quiet and cooperative and even helped pick up the props after practice.

"You were fierce!" Cadence said to Kenna as she headed off the mat.

"Thanks!" Kenna said. "So were you!"

"Well, I didn't just sprain my ankle!" Cadence answered.

Kelley couldn't stand it anymore. She stepped forward and stood between Kenna and the locker room. There was a moment of silence as she and Kenna stood face to face and everyone else just looked on.

Kelley took a deep breath and spoke. "I sorry I hurt your ankle, Kenna. You know it was an accident, right?"

Nobody was prepared for what came next. Kenna began to cry. She brought her hands up to her face and then rushed into the locker room. The girls followed her into the locker room. She sat sobbing on the bench. The girls took turns patting her on the back.

Kelley looked at Cadence, not sure how to stand or what to say. She suddenly felt incredibly clumsy like her arms were way too long for her body. "I'm sorry!" she insisted, not sure what was going on.

"No," Kenna finally choked out. "I'm not crying because of the sprain..."

There was silence as they waited for her to say more.

"Then why?" Cadence finally asked.

Kenna struggled to start speaking, as if she were searching for her courage. But once she began, it was as if she couldn't stop.

"I knew it was an accident all along—that you wouldn't hurt me on purpose. But I pretended I thought you had, because I was freaked out by your routine... you were so good and you just started..." Kenna's shoulders shook up and down as she spoke. "I felt so jealous that you could be as good as me... maybe even better... and on top of that, everybody likes you!"

The girls stood silent, shocked.

"I was really surprised when you stepped on my foot and it really did swell up but I was faking how much it hurt or how much damage was actually done."

"So..." Cadence searched for words. "What changed? Why are you telling us this?"

"Because I'm really sorry," she said plainly and then she looked at each girl's face. "It all got totally out of hand. And then my mom... I had no idea she was going to insist Gail kick Kelley off the team because of the Code of Conduct and the bullying thing. And then on the way home, she just kept ranting about it all. She wouldn't stop. And I realized something I've never realized before..."

Kelley sat down next to Kenna and put her arm around her. It seemed to give Kenna the support she needed. Her voice became calmer as she continued talking.

"My mom is the bully."

Kelley actually heard one of the girls gasp though she wasn't sure which one.

"She's always been a bully," she continued, "and I don't want to be like her."

Kenna lifted her head to speak one last time. "Can you forgive me?" Her gaze went from face to face as she looked at every girl.

Perhaps they were struck silent by the amazing change in Kenna or maybe they just weren't sure they could trust it. But either way, it took the girls a moment to be able, one by one, to look Kenna in the eye and nod.

"Of course, Kenna," Cadence finally said. "You're our teammate. We forgive you."

****

That night as Kelly lay in bed trying to visualize her part in the group routine for the competition, all she could see was Kenna's face—smiling. What an amazing transformation! It seemed almost too good to be true, but Kelley wanted desperately for the change to be real—and to last.

Her phone buzzed. Cadence.

"Um, so, what was that about?"

Kelley started typing madly. "I know, right?! Totally different person!"

"Think it will last?"

"Dunno" Kelley typed back. "Hope so!"

"Poor Kenna!"

Kelley agreed. How horrible to have a mom who's a bully. "Must be awful," she texted. "I mean, we're so lucky."

"Our moms are kind of great" Cadence texted.

"The BEST!!!"

"See you tomorrow?" Cadence asked.

"Of course!!" Kelley responded. "Fingers crossed the new Kenna is at the gym!"

"Fingers crossed!!!!!"

Kelley pulled open her drawer to put her phone away for the night and then changed her mind.

Before going to sleep, Kelley sent one last text. This one was to her mom, who was probably in the kitchen right now making herself a mug of tea before bed, kindly putting away the last of the dishes, and making sure everything was all set for the next day. Definitely NOT being a bully.

"Thank you!" Kelley typed. She didn't know when her mom would get it, but she wanted to make sure her mom knew how grateful she was to have her for a mother.

Her phone quickly buzzed.

"You're very welcome. For what?"

Kelley smiled at her mom's message and quickly typed back, "For being the best mom in the whole world!"

"Hard not to be when you've got the best daughter!" The sound of her mom's voice startled Kelley.

"I love you, mom," Kelley said as her mom walked over and sat beside her on the bed.

"I love you, too, Kell. I love you, too."

CHAPTER 18

Kelley and her teammates were standing in the locker room they'd been assigned. They were all in uniform and the rumble of the crowd in the bleachers could be heard even from where they stood.

"This is just the beginning!" Gail said to the girls as they waited for every word of encouragement they could get. "You each have to go out there and leave it on the mat, but whatever happens today, you must look at this as the first step in a long journey of becoming the very best rhythm gymnast you can be! So take a deep breath, remember your training, then clear your mind and have a wonderful time!"

The girls broke into applause and cheers as they headed out the door toward the wide-open space of the gym with the large performance mats taking center stage. They walked in a straight line and moved in unison until they got to the bench assigned to them. They each wore their hair pulled back tight into a pony tail and their make-up was thick and stage-ready just like for all the other gymnastics competitions. Even the butterflies in Kelley's stomach felt the same. The only thing different was the turquoise and purple leotards they all wore, some with bras, some without.

Kelley looked at the event order taped to the wall near where she was sitting. Even though she dreamed of standing on a gold medal podium some day, today she was glad she was competing as a Level 5 gymnast. It was a lower level than she'd been in as an artistic gymnast but for her first time competing in Rhythmic, this was a good plan!

Cadence, Kenna, and Heather were higher, but of course, they'd all been doing this for years! Kelley was also glad that in this smaller meet and thanks to her lower level, she didn't have to compete with all the equipment in her very first competition. She could just focus on her Hoop routine, the compulsory Ball routine and of course, the Group routine with the Hoop. That was enough for one competition!

She studied the schedule. It was complicated with so many different events. It would be easy to accidentally miss a performance if you weren't paying close attention to what was happening on the different mats. She wanted to be sure she knew when Cadence would be up with her Ball routine. She didn't want to miss any of her teammates' big events—Heather with the Ribbon, Alexa with Ball, and even Kenna with Clubs.

The Group competition came last. Kelley was glad she'd have her individual events out of the way by the time the Group started. She didn't want to worry about anything but doing her best for the team!

Before she could even scan the crowd in search of her mom, the opening announcements were made and the competition began. She watched Cadence step out on to the mat. Her confidence was inspiring and seemed to demand attention. It felt as though Cadence had the crowd following her before she'd even begun. She held the shiny red ball securely in her right hand as she hit her opening pose. Then as her music began to play, Cadence moved swiftly into her first sequence of skills that included a high toss as she spiraled around and a series of dribbles as she showed off her incredible extension. Kelley felt so proud to have a friend who performed so perfectly under pressure. She leaped and kicked her back leg up so that it touched her head as she executed a mid-air kind of backbend. She never once bobbled the ball. Her control was absolute all the way through to her final pose, which she hit with a huge smile on her face.

The team burst into a great round of cheers and shouts as Cadence ran off the mat smiling.

"Amazing!" Kelley cheered. "You were perfect!"

"Hardly perfect," Cadence laughed, "but it felt pretty good!"

There wasn't time to dwell on any performance too long as the events came one after another, very quickly. There were at least half a dozen teams competing and more than one performance happening at any given time. It was so important to not get distracted.

Kelley focused her attention on her breathing as she watched Priya take the mat, the rope doubled over and held in her left hand. Kelley tried to release the tension that was sneaking into her shoulders. She watched Priya control the rope as she pirouetted across the mat. Kelley was still working on her consistency with rope and so was very impressed at Priya's ability to seem so relaxed and yet so in control throughout the entire routine. The rope was as long as Priya was tall and she moved from fast jumps over the rope to tosses that seemed impossibly difficult to time and she hit every mark. In practice, she had struggled at times to maintain control, but didn't seem to have any problems today.

Priya is like Jamie, Kelley thought. *Having an audience just makes her better.*

As the rest of the squad watched, Priya did a forward handspring leading the rope along behind her with her back leg.

Kelley held her breath as Priya spun the rope above her head like a lasso and then did a series of tumbles and tosses.

She ended her routine with a particularly complicated series of tumbles and leaps before sticking her final pose, rope extended between her outstretched foot and arm.

The team ran to the edge of the mat as she ended her routine. They crowded around her and gave her a group hug for her great performance.

"That was so much fun!" Priya said. "And my leo stayed on!"

Kelley laughed, grateful for her teammate's sense of humor.

"Are you ready?" Gail asked and it took Kelley a moment to realize she was talking to her.

"Yes!" Kelley answered as she clenched and unclenched her fists.

"You're up!" Gail smiled. She gave Kelley's shoulder a quick squeeze.

"Have a good time!" Cadence whispered in her ear as she grabbed her on the way to the mat.

"Go, Kelley!" she heard her teammates shouting out support.

As she stood waiting for her music to fill the air, Kelley felt a calm take over her body. She recognized the sensation. It was the way she always felt in the second before the lights would come up when she used to dance ballet. That moment in the dark when all you could do is wait for the show to begin was when Kelley knew whether her head was in the right place. There were two choices in that moment: panic or trust the hard work. It was the moment when she would know whether she trusted herself to succeed.

She lowered her body into her starting position, hoop raised high above her head.

As she waited on the mat in her first rhythmic competition to begin, Kelley realized she totally trusted herself to succeed. She'd worked hard and she could do this. The music began, she thrust the hoop into the air with her foot and was off to a routine that hit every skill it was supposed to. Kelley didn't think about catching the hoop; she only thought to extend her arm. The hoop finally felt like a part of her body. The hoop moved closer and further away but it was always under her control. At one point she did a handstand and slowly moved her legs in through the hoop, bending her body backward as she would do on the beam until she was once again standing, the hoop spinning in her outstretched hand. Then she rolled it around her head, behind her shoulder, and then across her chest as she'd done over Thanksgiving with the soccer ball. She followed this move with a grand jeté and tossed the hoop high up into the air, confident that it would be there when she reached back out for it. And as the hoop fell into her hand for the last time in the routine, Kelley couldn't help but smile. She had just had the best time she'd had in a long time. Rhythm really was everything she loved about ballet and everything she loved about gymnastics all rolled into one great sport!

It felt like a brand new competition once that first performance was under Kelley's belt. Now she could really enjoy watching all the great gymnasts. She could really take in all there was to learn by watching girls who were much further along in their skills than she was.

It was even an education to watch how the girls presented themselves when the individual awards were announced. Even the way they carried themselves with near-perfect posture, heads held high, shoulders back, combined things she knew from ballet and gymnastics.

It was a thrill to see so many of the First Place awards go to her teammates. Cadence took first place for both the Ball and Floor. Kenna took first with Clubs. Priya placed first with rope. Kelley didn't place, but it didn't even bother her. She'd done a great job for her first Rhythmic competition.

"I'm very proud of you," Gail said as they watched the other girls accepting their awards. "That was a huge first step for you today!"

"I know," Kelley agreed. "I got through all my skills without a mistake and I really felt like the hoop was a part of me!"

Gail nodded and gave her a quick hug.

"Good job," Kenna said as she walked past Kelley on her way to their next event.

Kelley caught her breath, surprised for a moment. *I guess the new Kenna is planning to stick around for a while,* Kelley thought. *Awesome.*

"Ribbons and medals will follow!" Gail proclaimed and they gave each other a high five.

With individual awards over, it was time for the girls to hit the floor with their group routine. Kelley joined Cadence, Priya, Heather, and Kenna as they held hands in a circle and looked into each other's eyes right before heading out to the place on the floor.

"Break a leg out there," Cadence whispered to her teammates.

"Break a leg," they each replied in turn.

"And thank you," said Kenna. "We're a great team!"

"Let's go, girls!" Gail cheered and the girls broke their circle and headed to their starting positions, each with a hoop balanced in a different way.

This was everything Kelley had missed during the time since she'd left soccer. She loved this moment when she was so completely connected to her teammates and they were all totally focused on the same thing.

The music started and each of the girls took their hoop and raised it above their heads. From there, they moved in a circle while pirouetting in smaller circles. They each lowered the hoops, one after another and jumped through them on their way to cartwheels and forward rolls that spread them out across the mat. Now they were in position to criss-cross each other in a series of jetés that included high hoop tosses, the last of which had them catching each other's hoops. It felt as though they were in total unison. As much as the hoop had felt like an extension of her body during her individual routine, now each girl felt as though the hoop was a part of the person. The girls were even breathing in unison.

So when Kenna's arm extended a beat later than everyone else's, it felt amazingly awkward. Kelley's attention was diverted for a split second so she saw when the hoop came down and missed Kenna's grasp. Kelley's eye went back to her own hoop just in time to catch her own. But it was already too late. Their perfect routine was no longer perfect. Kenna had dropped the hoop.

They were barely off the mat before Kelley heard sniffles behind her. She turned to see Kenna crying, her head held low. "We did great!" Heather said. "Why are you crying?"

"I dropped the hoop," Kenna whimpered. "I ruined our chances of placing."

"So you dropped the hoop," Cadence said, dismissing it as unimportant. "We still did a great job of working totally together."

"Right?" said Priya. "I don't think we've ever been that in-sync before!"

"Still," Kenna said, "I'm really sorry!"

"People make mistakes sometimes," Kelley said. "As long as you learn from them, it's all okay."

The team made a tight circle around Kenna. Kelley was amazed how bad she felt watching Kenna feel so upset. She never thought she would have so much compassion for the ex-bully, but this first competition and everything that had led up to it had really made them a team! They were bonded now and Kelley could just feel it—they were headed for great things!

CHAPTER 19

As applause rang out for the teams that placed first, second and third, Kelley joined in. It had been a great day of competition and she felt as though she had learned a year's worth of information in about three hours. Next time, she would really be ready to go after the competition and get herself on the podium!

She turned to study the crowd in the bleachers. She wanted to find her mom. But before she found her mom, her eyes fell on a group of girls all looking back at her—all wearing fuchsia and black.

The Kips! Kelley couldn't believe her eyes. All the Kips had shown up to watch her in her first Rhythmic competition. They broke out in an extra loud round of cheers when they realized Kelley had finally seen them.

"Kell, Kell, Hooray!" They shouted in unison. "Kell, Kell, Hooray!"

"That's so nice they all came," Cadence said as she turned in the direction of the cheering.

"I'm so glad I didn't know they were there!" Kelley laughed. "It would have made me even more nervous!"

"I'll say," Cadence laughed. "Did you see who's sitting next to Jamie?"

Kelley looked again and realized Donovan was waving at her too. "Uh, wow," she giggled. "No, I hadn't noticed that!"

"Seriously?" Cadence stared at her. "Who couldn't notice?" She tilted her head very slightly in the direction of Donovan.

"Stop!" Kelley whispered, as if they might be heard over the cheering crowd.

She tried to wave back to Donovan as casually as possible but it was hard to contain her excitement. As if getting through her first competition cleanly wasn't enough, the official "Cutest Neighbor Ever!" was there to see it!

"Go talk to them!" Cadence nudged her. "And him!"

Kelley worked her way through the crowd until she got to Jamie and the rest of the team.

"Soooo good!" Jamie said as she gave Kelley a huge hug.

"That looks really fun! And you look so great doing it!" Bethany added.

"I'm so happy I didn't drop anything!" Kelley laughed. She was trying not to look at Donovan but she was having trouble focusing on what her friends were saying.

"You were totally in charge," Donovan said and Kelley had to look at him. He was looking at her with total admiration on his face.

"Thanks," she said. "I was surprised to see you here."

"Really?" he said. "Good surprise, I hope,"

Kelley giggled. It was fun to feel that she had his attention but she didn't like feeling as though she was ignoring her friends. She turned back to her old teammates.

"I would love to try this," Sara chirped.

"No way! We can't lose anyone else!" Jamie smiled. She turned to Kelley, "You obviously are doing what you're supposed to be doing, but that doesn't keep me from wishing you were still with the Kips!"

"It wasn't bad," said Nadia, trying to hold back a smile. "You know, for a *dance* performance."

Kelley smiled and rolled her eyes. Then she hugged all her friends. It was so good to see them. She hadn't realized just how much she had missed them. Kelley felt that old monster creeping up inside her. She wanted to do *everything*! Not just for the sport of it but because she loved all her different friends so much.

"I think he's waiting for you," Jamie whispered, gesturing very quietly toward Donovan.

Kelley turned to see that Donovan had stepped away from the

group a little bit and seemed to be hoping she might talk to him some more.

"Hold on a second," Kelley said and she stepped away from the team and walked over to where Donovan was waiting. The girls wandered away a bit, clearly trying to give Kelley some privacy.

"So what are you doing now?" Donovan asked, and it was clear he was hoping Kelley might want to spend some time with him. She knew she had to speak her mind or she would end up in a situation she wasn't comfortable being in.

"It was really great that you came," she started. "I really like you—as a friend—" she glanced up at his face and knew she had to keep talking.

"I'm so busy though—I mean, the truth is, I think I'm not ready for anything more than 'just friends,' you know?" She looked at him again and the smile was not quite so broad across his face, but there was still a sweetness to his expression.

"I want to stay really focused on my goals in gymnastics and in school and I think boys might be a little distracting!" It took a second, but then they both laughed a little bit. Donovan nodded.

"Yeah," he said. "I can understand that. Because I definitely find you distracting!"

Her stomach flipped in a strange combination of excitement and nerves. "We'll see each other up at the cottage though!" she said as her heart raced. "And you're totally welcome to hang out with us—as a group I mean—I think we're going for pizza tonight or ice cream or something."

He nodded and then she felt him leaning in ever so slightly. Was he going to kiss her good-bye? Kelley stepped back just a little, hoping he would stop.

"There she is!" Kelley heard her mother's voice and never had it sounded so sweet! She turned and gave her mother a huge, grateful hug.

"She's a champion in the making!" said Gail, who stood next to her mother. Jamie and Bethany suddenly returned and Cadence appeared along with them.

"That's exactly what I was just saying!" said Donovan.

Kelley shot him a look and punched him playfully on the arm. *Maybe in a year or two, she thought,* as she watched him walk over to talk to a Jamie. There was no denying the fact that he was one cute boy!

"So listen!" Bethany said, the only one not seeming to notice what had just happened with Donovan. "I found this cool camp online. It's in Portland and is run by some Cirque du Soleil trainers. You get to work with silks and ropes! I was thinking maybe you and I could try it next summer! Now that you're all into Rhythmic and ribbons and things."

There was a round of laughter once Bethany stopped talking. Her enthusiasm was wonderful and funny at the same time.

"Do you do gymnastics as fast as you talk?" Cadence asked with a warm smile.

"You can see for yourself," Kelley said. "I am bringing you to the Kips' first meet in January."

"Maybe you could come to the camp with us too!" Bethany exclaimed.

Kelley had never seen Bethany so upbeat and positive before. It only added to the warm feeling she felt welling up inside her. As the group made their way out of the gym, Kelly felt her different worlds finally coming together. She was on her way in a brand new challenge that she loved and she had all her friends and family coming along with her for the ride. She was doing exactly what she wanted to be doing. And she was exactly where she belonged!

ABOUT THE AUTHOR

April Adams has spent almost as much time upside down as right side up. As a competitive gymnast she led her University of Alabama team to the top of the podium and although her sights were never on the Olympics, after a degree in creative writing , April went as a journalist to the London games. April loves hiking, baking and spending time with her family in Utah.

Made in the USA
Middletown, DE
10 May 2016